THE GOSPEL FROM THE MOUNT

Baptist

Books by John Wick Bowman
Published by The Westminster Press

The Gospel from the Mount
The Drama of the Book of Revelation
Prophetic Realism and the Gospel
The Intention of Jesus

THE
GOSPEL
FROM THE
MOUNT

A New Translation and Interpretation of Matthew, Chs. 5 to 7

by

John Wick Bowman

and

Roland W. Tapp

Philadelphia

THE WESTMINSTER PRESS

Library of Congress Catalog Card Number: 57-9708

PRINTED IN THE UNITED STATES OF AMERICA

To
LOUISE AND HELEN
in loving appreciation

Contents

PREFACE

The contents of this little book represent an endeavor to popularize interpretations of the Sermon on the Mount that have been given over a period of some thirty years to students on three continents. Many of these students, therefore, will recognize familiar ground here. I hope that such students will find the book useful in presenting interpretations which they will recall to have been made in the attempt to understand the Greek idiom and the Aramaic lying behind it.

These chapters also present in substance the content of the Norton Lectures delivered at the Southern Baptist Theological Seminary in Louisville, Kentucky, in the spring of 1957. May I take occasion, therefore, to express my thanks to the Trustees and Faculty of the Seminary for their gracious invitation to deliver the course of lectures and more particularly for the stimulus that has occasioned the casting of these notes in the form of a book. I am not certain whether the Seminary authorities, in asking me to deliver the Norton Lectures at this time, realized that these lectures would be given exactly thirty years after the year which closed my own studies under that prince of teachers, Archibald Thomas Robertson. May I express the hope that this little volume may prove in some measure stimulating as were his classroom seminars.

Associated with me in the preparation of this volume has been Roland W. Tapp, Th.D., beloved student and research colleague, to whose arduous labors both on this book and on a

9

previous one I owe a debt of lasting gratitude. He is largely responsible for the notes and their scholarly contribution, as well as for an occasional paragraph in the text itself and much-needed criticism and encouragement throughout the preparation of the book. Our mutual thanks go also to Mrs. Tadashi Akaishi for her fine co-operation and expert service in typing.

The translation, or perhaps better the paraphrase, presented in this volume is original with the author. I have employed throughout the well-known Nestle text in its twenty-first edition of 1952. However, I have not refrained from departing from the text in favor of what I considered better readings or greater clarity. In the interpretation of the text, however, Scripture quotations frequently are made from the King James Version, the Revised Standard Version, or one of the modern English translations. I have employed the name of Matthew throughout, without intending thereby to express a judgment relative to the authorship of the First Gospel.

JOHN WICK BOWMAN

INTRODUCTION

Our Lord's Poetry

Our Lord was a master of the teaching craft. " Teacher" or " rabbi," the equivalent of our title " professor," was the principal term of address applied to Jesus Christ by his disciples (Matt. 26:25; Mark 4:38).[1] The crowd also called Jesus " rabbi " on occasion (Luke 12:13), and even his enemies so addressed him (Mark 12:14). As a master teacher, therefore, Jesus employed the three most up-to-date teaching methods of his day — namely, the sermon, the parable, and the poem. None of these was new in his time, since all of them were found in the Hebrew literature dating from the period of the prophets. The rabbis of his day still employed these three methods and Jesus took advantage of this common practice to present his message to the people.

1. *The Sermon.* The so-called "Sermon on the Mount," which we are about to study, is perhaps the best-known example of a sermon preached by our Lord. Numerous parallels, as we shall see, exist between this sermon and that called the " Sermon on a Level Place" (Luke 6:17). But a number of other sermons preached by Jesus also are to be found in the Gospels, and as has often been remarked, Matthew's Gospel appears to be a narrative interspersed with from five to seven of such sermons. Other examples are his " Charge to the Twelve " at their first sending forth in ch. 10, the "Parables of the Kingdom" in ch. 13, and the "Discourse on the Last Things " in chs. 24 and 25.

2. *The Parable.* Under the heading of " parable " are to be included not only the so-called story parables but also the doom
song, aphorism, allegory, and acted parable, all of which Jesus
employed as a master teacher. Examples of the story parable
are almost too numerous to require illustration. T. W. Manson
suggests that " after allowing for doublets there is a total of
sixty-five parables." [2] Adolf Jülicher in his monumental work on
our Lord's parables makes the count fifty-three in all.[3] Many
scholars think it somewhat doubtful that Jesus ever employed
the allegory.[4] However, in some of the explanations of his parables, our Lord certainly does appear to allegorize, as for example, in the case of the parable of the sower (Mark 4:10–20), and
John's Gospel is noteworthy for its allegories, as for example
that of the vine and the branches in ch. 15.[5]

Professor Manson has also suggested that there is no clear
case of the doom song, or taunt song, in the teaching of Jesus.[6]
To the present writer, however, it would appear that there are
at least two clear examples of this literary phenomenon. The
first of these is found in his so-called " Upbraiding of the Cit-
ies " in Luke 10:13–15 and Matt. 11:20–24; the second is in his
" Weeping Over Jerusalem " in Luke 13:34 f. and Matt. 23:37–
39. The aphorisms discoverable in our Lord's teaching are almost innumerable. Examples are the following: " You are the
light of the world " (Matt. 5:14); " Judge not, that you be not
judged " (Matt. 7:1); " The Sabbath was made for man, not
man for the Sabbath; so the Son of Man is Lord even of the
Sabbath " (Mark 2:27 f.); " Truly, truly, I say to you, I am the
door of the sheep " (John 10:7). Jesus' teaching in all the Gospels is liberally sprinkled with examples of such aphoristic sayings. One gains the impression that he was a master in uttering
such at a moment's notice. Everyone is acquainted with some
friend who is good at repartee. Jesus' method of repartee would
undoubtedly have been the aphorism.

The so-called acted parable or emblem prophecy is scarcely
to be reckoned as a literary device. As a parable in action, however, it certainly ranks as a teaching method. In such emblem

prophecy either the acted parable itself or its author was intended as a " sign " or a memorial of the working of God in the midst of his people. That our Lord consciously employed such acted parables as signs or memorials there can be no doubt. Examples of this are his selection of the Twelve as a memorial of the presence and saving activity of the remnant, his entry into Jerusalem as a memorial to the people of Israel and particularly to the rulers that the Messiah had come, the Lord's Supper as a sign of his approaching death as the Suffering Servant, the foot washing as a memorial of the humility properly belonging to the Servant, and the cleansing of the Temple as a sign of his lordly relation to it. (Matt. 10:2 ff.; Mark 11:1–10; 14:22–25; John 13:12–17; Mark 11: 15–18, 27–33.) There can be no doubt also that his miracles were intended as " signs " in this high sense of a memorial that God was at work among his people.

3. *The Poem.* If our Lord was a master in the field of aphorism and parable, he was a poet of no mean ability. It is to the lasting credit of Aramaic scholarship that this fact has been uncovered during the past generation. And one is constrained to believe that conviction on the part of scholars of Jesus' ability to write or to compose poetry is almost in direct proportion to one's knowledge of the Aramaic tongue. Wellhausen and C. F. Burney were the first to develop this thesis to a marked degree. Notable among Aramaic scholars who have made contributions in this field since their day are Friedrich Schulthess, T. W. Manson, and Matthew Black.[7] It is not too much to hope, perhaps, that we are now on the threshold of a new understanding of our Lord's teaching as a result of the laborious efforts of such scholars.

Semitic poetry is characterized by four aspects, namely, by rhyme, rhythm, parallelism, and word play. We are, of course, quite familiar with the first two of these characteristics from our own English literature and they need no illustration. The phenomenon of parallelism, however, is not so commonly found in English poetry although it is not entirely absent. The word refers to a sort of balanced structure between the two halves of

a line or verse, or between verses, in the original Aramaic which
Jesus spoke, as well as in other Semitic languages. Semitic
scholars have distinguished at least the following five types of
parallelism:

1. *Synonymous*
    " O Lord, who shall sojourn in thy tent?
    Who shall dwell on thy holy hill? "

(Ps. 15:1.)

    " Ask — it will be given you;
    Seek — you will find;
    Knock — it will be opened to you."

(Matt. 7:7.)

2. *Antonymous*
    " Sacrifice and offering thou dost not desire;
    But thou hast given me an open ear."

(Ps. 40:6.)

    " Man shall not live by bread alone,
    But by every word that proceeds from the mouth of God."

(Matt. 4:4; Deut. 8:3.)

3. *Synthetic*
    " I love the Lord, because he has heard
    My voice and my supplications.
    Because he inclined his ear to me,
    Therefore I will call on him as long as I live."

(Ps. 116:1–2.)

    " Blessed are you poor,
    For yours is the Kingdom of God."

(Luke 6:20.)

4. *Step Parallelism*
    " O Lord, open thou my lips,
    And my mouth shall show forth thy praise.
    For thou hast no delight in sacrifice;
    Were I to give a burnt offering, thou wouldst not be
        pleased.
    The sacrifice acceptable to God is a broken spirit;
    A broken and contrite heart, O God, thou wilt not de-
        spise."

(Ps. 51:15–17.)

    " He that receiveth you, receiveth me;
    And he that receiveth me, receiveth him that sent me."

(Matt. 10:40.)

5. *Strophic Parallelism*

" No one sews a piece of unshrunk cloth
  On an old garment;
  If he does, the patch tears away from it,
  The new from the old,
  And a worse tear is made.
  And no one puts new wine into old wineskins;
  If he does, the wine will burst the skins,
  And the wine is lost, and so are the skins;
  But new wine is for fresh skins."

(Mark 2:21 f.) [8]

As will readily appear from a study of the above examples,
the synonymous and the antonymous types of parallelism are
characterized by the two parts of the line or verse standing in
relation to one another in a way suggested by the terms employed. In the case of synthetic parallelism the second part of
the verse or the second line serves to complete the meaning of
the first. Step parallelism is characterized by the first half of the
second line taking up the second half of the first, the third the
second half of the second, etc., as the term " step " suggests.
The term " strophic parallelism " is an invention of T. W. Manson and by it he means a lengthy passage in which a number
of the other types of parallelism are found in conjunction.

The fourth characteristic of Semitic poetry that we find Jesus
employing is that of word play. We are familiar with this phenomenon in our own English literature. The pun is perhaps the
commonest example with us. It was Samuel Johnson, I believe,
who was noted in his day for this " lowest form of wit " and
when asked to make a pun he instantly replied, " Upon what
subject? " Word play of this sort involving alliteration or the
repetition of certain consonants throughout a series of lines or
verses was a marked feature of the poetry of the Semites. Julius
Wellhausen, C. C. Torrey, T. W. Manson, Matthew Black, and
their associates, have proved beyond doubt that " when we
translate the Greek of the sayings of Jesus and of some of the
nondominical sayings " of the Gospels " back into simple Palestinian Aramaic, . . . examples of this formal element in the

poetry of the Gospels come to light." [9]

Examples of all these phenomena characterizing Aramaic poetry occur in the teaching of Jesus and often at the most unlikely places.[10] I have long felt with Professor Manson that " it is much to be desired that in editions of the text of the Gospels, whether Greek or English, the poetical pieces should be printed as such." [11] It is to be deplored, one believes, that most of our modern translations do not exhibit Jesus' teaching in its poetical form where such occurs. It does appear strange that the Old Testament translators are more prepared to cast the writings of the Hebrew prophets in poetical form than are our New Testament translators in dealing with the teaching of Jesus.

PRACTICAL VALUE ATTACHING TO THE RECOGNITION OF JESUS' POETRY

The practical value attaching to the recognition of a piece of literature as poetry will be apparent upon a moment's reflection. Particularly is this the case in the matter of the parallelism to which we have referred. For when the parallel structure is recognized, it serves to aid us in the interpretation of a given passage. The opposite sides of the parallel or the several couplets or lines which are in parallel construction serve to define one another, either as synonyms or antonyms or in some other characteristic manner. An example of this will suffice. In Isa., ch. 51, the following couplet serves as a refrain throughout the chapter:

"My deliverance draws near speedily,
My salvation has gone forth."

(Vs. 5, 6, 8.)

For "deliverance" the older versions read "righteousness." Whether we read "deliverance" or "righteousness," in any case the word clearly stands over against "salvation" in the second part of the couplet. If, therefore, we do not understand the way in which the prophet is using the word "salvation" or "righteousness" (or "deliverance"), the one side of the equa-

tion serves to define the other. That is to say, for the Second
Isaiah " righteousness " or " deliverance " meant " to be saved,"
and similarly " to be saved " meant in some sense to receive
God's deliverance or righteousness. The discovery of this phenomenon is of the greatest significance for interpreting any
passage, as will readily be apparent, and is of real help in our
understanding of the teaching of the Sermon on the Mount.

For another reason also it is advantageous to know that Jesus
taught his disciples, and to some extent the multitudes as well,
in the manner of a poet. Some years ago B. S. Easton attempted
to defend the thesis that Jesus not only taught his disciples in
the form of poetry but that he required them as well to memorize his poems.[12] One does not readily see how such a thesis
could be demonstrated and the present writer has never been
convinced of its truth. However, Easton's thesis is in my judgment an error in the right direction. One would restate his thesis as follows: Jesus taught his disciples in the form of poetry
because this is the form of literature of all primitive peoples and
to memorize poetry is far easier than to memorize prose.

In modern India and for centuries past there has existed the
equivalent of the medieval European bard. The present writer
has on numerous occasions heard this bard playing and chanting the great Indian epics known as *Ramayana* and *Mahab-
harata* to large audiences in the Indian villages. One knew that
approximately 95 per cent of the Indian villagers were entirely
illiterate. The bard himself was in many cases also. A notable
example of this phenomenon was an utterly illiterate bard who
in the early days of the Swaraj (nationalistic) movement used
to travel about through the villages of the United Provinces,
gathering audiences of thousands and chanting to them as he
thrummed the old epics of his people on one of the Indian in-
struments. This bard became a center of unrest in that province
and his influence in the Gandhi movement was widespread.
After the bard left the village one heard both children and
adults chanting large portions of these epics which they had
learned through the medium of the ear alone! [13]

Our Lord, therefore, was well advised to employ this useful medium in his teaching. No doubt in many cases the exact words of his teaching have been preserved to us on this account. In the past some people have imagined that Jesus' disciples may have taken down what he had to say in shorthand, but we are unacquainted with any such medium for the Aramaic tongue in which he spoke. It is far more likely that the poetic form of much of his teaching lent itself to easy memorization.

The Gospel of the Kingdom

Jesus went about, then, in all Galilee —
  in their synagogues teaching and preaching the gospel of the
    Kingdom,
  healing every disease, every malady among the people.
His fame, moreover, spread through all Syria —
  so they fetched to him all who were ill,
  those afflicted with various sicknesses and torments:
  the demon-possessed, the moon-struck, the paralytic,
  and he healed them all.
Great crowds, therefore, accompanied him —
  from Galilee, the Decapolis, Jerusalem, Judea, and from across
    the Jordan.
When, then, he saw the crowds, he went up the mountain,
  and he had no sooner sat down than his disciples gathered
    themselves around him.
So, opening his mouth, he taught them as follows —
                                        (Matt. 4:23 to 5:2.)

A proper understanding of the Sermon on the Mount depends to a large extent on our noting where it is intended by Matthew to begin. This is clearly at ch. 4:23 and not as in our modern Bibles at ch. 5:1. Accordingly, the passage just quoted begins at this point.

Our modern chapter and verse divisions are not of ancient origin. The division into chapters goes back only to Cardinal Hugo de San Caro (a Spaniard) in the year 1238. Our verse divisions date only from Robert Estienne (a French scholar), who made them in 1551. Some confusion results in our understanding of the text in view of the fact that these two Continental scholars at times were misled in their endeavors to create a chapter-verse series of divisions.

In the present instance the result has been disquieting. For some Bible students have misinterpreted our Lord's intention in his teaching by reason of the fact that the Sermon on the Mount begins with ch. 5:1 rather than ch. 4:23. They have supposed that we have in the Sermon on the Mount a " New Law." The parallelism has been pointed out between the work of Moses and that of Jesus somewhat as follows: Moses went up into Mount Sinai and returned with the Old Law for Israel; similarly, Jesus went up into a mountain and gave to his disciples a New Law. How misleading this parallelism is can be readily discerned in the conclusion which is sometimes stated, namely, that inasmuch as Christians are not under the law but under grace or the gospel, therefore the Sermon on the Mount is not relevant to them! [1]

When, however, we discover that this chapter division was not in accordance with the mind of the author of the Gospel, the difficulty immediately disappears. For it is obvious that in ch. 4:23 Matthew is presenting us with the true subject of the Sermon, namely, " the gospel of the Kingdom." And the paragraph represented by ch. 4:23 through ch. 5:2 is intended as an introductory statement on the author's part to indicate, first, the theme of our Lord's Sermon on the Mount and, secondly, the fact that at the time he was at the height of his popularity, crowds following about him from all sides. It surely behooves us then to discover in what sense and to what degree this Sermon may be described as " The Gospel of the Divine Lordship or Sovereignty." And now that we are alerted to the matter, it will not be difficult, one imagines, to discover the gospel from the first word onward in the Sermon.

Two other items are outstanding in the author's prologue to the Sermon. These are, first, that Jesus began his teaching and preaching ministry in the synagogues of his people. This had been the worship and educational center for perhaps a hundred

and fifty or more years before his time. It has been suggested
that the universal education of Jewish boys was the creation of
Simeon ben Shatah, whose date is about the beginning of the
first century before Christ.[2] The synagogue as a worship center
had existed long before this date and its worship service had
been cultivated by the Pharisees more especially. In consequence, the synagogue was the natural center for our Lord to
begin his teaching and preaching ministry as was, of course, also
true in later days in the case of his great apostle, Paul
(Acts 13:5).

The other fact that should not escape our attention is that
noted in ch. 5:1, that the reason for Jesus' going up the mountain was to escape the crowds and that the Sermon was directed
not to the crowds, although they may have been sitting on the
fringe, but rather to his disciples. It was Jesus' custom throughout his ministry thus to direct his straightforward teaching to his
disciples, whether in prose or poetry. On the other hand, in general he addressed the multitudes in parables (Mark 4:10–12).

" His fame, moreover, spread through all Syria —
            so they fetched to him all who were ill,
            those afflicted with various sicknesses and torments:
            the demon-possessed, the moon-struck, the paralytic,
            and he healed them all."
                                    (Matt. 4:24.)

The terms " demon-possessed " and " moon-struck " require a
word of comment. These terms represent the popular beliefs of
the day regarding certain types of illness which we would asso-
ciate with epilepsy. It was no part of the function of the writers
of Scripture, as this was determined by the inspiring Spirit of
God, to correct such popular beliefs. Indeed, had such correc-
tion been attempted in those times it would have outraged the
sensibilities of the readers of the Scriptures. It is arguable certainly that the Scripture writers employed these terms quite
loosely as we ourselves do today. And in any case, we are not as
Christians constrained to accept the popular beliefs of twenty
centuries ago. Moreover, it is not always easy to discover what

those beliefs were. The translation given above — " the demon-possessed, the moon-struck, the paralytic " — represents a literal rendering of the Greek. The Palestinian Syriac, however, which gives us a text more closely than the Greek representing the original Aramaic of the Evangelist, reads here: " both those afflicted by demons and the daughters of vigilance over them and the paralytic." Similarly, the Peshitta Syriac for " moon-struck " has " the sons of the housetops." All these expressions are no doubt endeavors to refer to semidivine or demonic beings with which popular fancy peopled the universe. Jesus in his teaching and preaching was never concerned to correct the popular views of his day on such fringe topics. His great concern was to teach and preach the gospel of the Kingdom in a manner intelligible to his generation. Surely this should be our concern today.[3]

The Two Sermons

In the Gospels of Matthew and Luke there are to be found at approximately this point two sermons preached by our Lord. We have already referred to these in the introduction as the " Sermon on the Mount " and the " Sermon on a Level Place." These two sermons to a large extent overlap and where they do so the overlapping material is ordinarily assigned to a common source designated as " Q." Where they fail to overlap — and such material is in all cases to be found in Matthew only — this is usually assigned to a source termed " M." The lay reader is referred to the note in the appendix which refers to available literature for a clarification of the meaning of " source " and of the two symbols to which reference has just been made.[4]

Another way of saying this is that Matthew found in the sources available to him two sermons of our Lord which he combined in one. This solution of the problem before us is perhaps acceptable to most scholars working in the field. It is, however, possible that Jesus himself combined materials from two sermons which he had preached and that Matthew found the " Q " and " M " sermons combined when they came into his

hands. Several phenomena connected with a critical analysis of
the materials have suggested to the present writer that the latter
solution is the more likely. In a book of this type, however, this
conclusion can only be stated without the demonstration that
would be required to convince the reader.[5]

Since it may be of service to the lay reader to orient himself
to the similarities and differences between the " Q " and " M "
sermons, the following brief description of them is offered. Each
sermon appears to begin with four Beatitudes — " Q " with
numbers 1, 2, 4, and 9 as they appear in Matthew (i.e., Matt.
5:3, 4, 6, 11 f.; Luke 6:20–23); " M " with numbers 5, 6, 7, and
8 as found in Matthew (i.e., Matt. 5:7–10). Each of these series
of Beatitudes comes to the same end. Each expresses the
thought that the realization of the Kingdom of God in human
life effects an inward transformation of the personality and
character.

It seems clear that in the Beatitudes the two sources, " Q "
and " M," are at one in giving us Jesus' own analysis of the
meaning of his Marcan saying, " The Kingdom of God is at
hand; repent, and believe in the gospel " (Mark 1:15). He
meant by this saying to call men to wholehearted allegiance to
God's rule over their lives, and further that this would eventu-
ate in an inward transforming experience resulting in the willingness to undergo vicarious suffering on behalf of (or, as a part
of) the people of God, the " redemptive community." In other
words, to achieve mature personality in Jesus' teaching is, like
him, to acquire that toughness with reference to the world and
that ability to stand alone against the world's inducements
which we call " character." And had our Lord given us a definition of that term, it is safe to say that he would have defined
it as the " image of God " acquired by the true disciple through
commitment to the will of God and through the suffering which
one making that commitment must be prepared to undergo in
an imperfect and sinful world.

In the " Q " sermon the Beatitudes were succeeded by a series of woes corresponding to them and directed against the

failure to commit oneself to the Kingdom (Luke 6:24–26).
These in turn were followed by a section on loving and doing
good to one's fellow men (vs. 27–45), whose theme is found in
v. 36: " Be merciful, even as your Father is merciful." By means
of various parables it was suggested that social righteousness
would be achieved in the world when men were made right at
the core of personality — when, in other words, they had acquired character (vs. 39–45) — for " the good man out of the
good treasure of his heart produces good, and the evil man out
of his evil treasure produces evil; for out of the abundance of
the heart his mouth speaks " (v. 45). Here " heart " is used
(after the manner of the Hebrew psychology) for the entire inner or higher side of a man's nature. Finally the " Q " sermon
closed with the parable of the house on the rock and that on the
earth (or sand, vs. 46–49), in which the picture of two individuals is seen. One has failed through lack of commitment, and the
other has achieved through wholehearted allegiance and consecration to the sovereignty of God.

In " M," the Beatitude call to commitment was followed by
an analysis of human personality and the teaching that it is
sacred at every point and must be reverenced and cultivated.
The teaching is divided into five headings: (a) reverence for
personality as such and consequent desisting from anger against
another's person (Matt. 5:21–26); (b) equality of the female
personality and the necessity of reverencing it even in thought
(vs. 27–32); (c) reverence for the intellect (or truth, its standard) and the requirement that a man's word be as good as his
bond (vs. 33–37); (d) reverence for the will and the willingness
to merge one's interests in those of the group (vs. 38–42); and
(e) reverence for the emotional life and the loving of men for
their own good quite apart from anything lovable which may
appear to be in them, even as God loves men without distinction (vs. 43–48). " M " also contained a section on true religion whose theme was a call to sincerity in man's relations with
God (ch. 6:1–8, 16–18).

Each sermon, then, had as its theme the achievement of character or moral personality through reverencing it in others and through merging one's interests in those of the community. In both sermons the thesis is that they who lose their lives will save them, a theme on which our Lord dwelt on more than one occasion, as both Mark (ch. 8:35) and " Q " (Luke 9:24) bear witness. The Christian, then, individually and as a member of the church of Christ, is to partake of his Lord's Spirit, to accept his evaluation of human personality in terms of moral character (the image of God) as this is achieved through the powerful inner working of the divine Word, and to follow him in total surrender to the will of God and so in apparent loss of what paradoxically can only be won by abandoning.

A. TRAVELING THE CHRISTIAN WAY

CHAPTER I

Portrait of a Christian — On the Way

God's gift to you who know your spiritual poverty —
the Kingdom of God is for you!

God's grace for you penitent —
you shall find forgiveness!

God's blessing on you serene —
you shall possess the land!

God's boon to you hungry and thirsty for righteousness —
you shall find satisfaction!

(Matt. 5:3–6.)

The Beatitudes which open the Sermon on the Mount, in the form presented to us in Matthew's Gospel at any rate, appear to represent an original Aramaic poem in two stanzas of four verses each. Stanza one of this poem — the four verses before us — has as its theme "The Upward Way of Christian Experience." The intimate second person — as the stanza appears at Luke 6:20–23 — accords well with the fact that in both the Matthean and Lucan forms the aim appears to be to portray the spiritual progress of a "son of the Kingdom" along lines laid down in the prophetic writings of the Old Testament Scriptures.

The various elements of this stanza represent a collection of scattered references from The Psalms and from Deutero-Isaiah, but as here arranged these manifest a genuine progress in the development of a type of personality. This development, we are given to understand, is a mobile portrait of the true follower of

Jesus Christ. We are not to suppose, therefore, that the Beatitudes speak of separate types of persons, as though the " spiritually poor," the " penitent," the " serene," and the rest represent
distinct individuals. Rather, as we shall see, the stanza is intended to portray the development of a single type of personality or character, whose salvation depends upon his successively
enjoying the experiences to which each of the Beatitudes in turn
witnesses.[1]

As was remarked in the prologue above, the theme of this
Sermon is grace or gospel, and not law. This begins to appear
from the first word onward. The word " blessed " opening each
of the Beatitudes (in the Greek, *makarios*) is clearly intended
to constitute the Beatitude a benediction whereby the blessing
it contains is conferred by God upon the type of character it
portrays, even as the corresponding " woe " in Luke 6:24-26 is
intended as God's judgment of doom upon the opposite type.
This thought is in accord with the teaching of Scripture as a
whole, to the effect that ultimately blessing is conferred by God
alone upon man. In some languages this fact is made graphic by
reason of the adjective " blessed " having to be rendered as a
passive participle — that is, as " having been blessed." The Arabic is of this character, where the word " blessed " is rendered
by *mubarrak*, a passive participle meaning literally " having
been blessed." In the Greek also the adjective *makarios* is a
predicate one, and it would be quite legitimate to translate each
Beatitude after the fashion: " The poor in spirit are blessed
because . . ."[2]

With a view to indicating the above facts graphically, we have
paraphrased the adjective *makarios* in each case by a different
noun and prefixed the word " God's " to show the source of the
blessing in each case. All this is to say that the Beatitudes severally announce God's blessing upon certain stages attained in
the development of the personality of the Christian pilgrim on
the upward way.

It should be noted, too, that the nature of the blessing is defined in the second member of the Beatitude in each case.

Needless to say, the blessings contemplated in the Beatitudes can by no means be expressed in English by the word or concept "happiness." Proceeding as they do from God, they partake of his character and are on a high moral and spiritual level, as we shall immediately note.[3] In the meantime, in accord with what has already been said about the parallel structure of Aramaic poetry, it should be noted that each of the eight Beatitudes in this poem conforms to the pattern of what we have called "synthetic" parallelism. That is to say, the second line of each Beatitude contains mention of a blessing which completes the promise or pronouncement made in the first line.

Let us look now at each Beatitude in this first stanza of the poem in turn.

Beatitude One. Realization

> "God's gift to you who know your spiritual poverty —
> the Kingdom of God is for you!"
>
> (Matt. 5:3.)

Modern interpreters have long recognized the fact that the keynote of this first Beatitude is "realization." Moffatt, for example, translates: "Blessed are those who feel poor in spirit!"; Goodspeed has: "Blessed are those who feel their spiritual need"; and Canon Wade: "Happy are those who are feeling spiritual need." The reason for this unanimity is Matthew's stress upon poverty "in spirit." Matthew's thought here requires to be explained; for Luke in the same passage does not contain the phrase in question (Luke 6:20). The conception has a long history behind it.

The "poor" man (*'ani*) in Israel had from time immemorial been represented in the law and the prophetic writings as an object of God's special care, and therefore was to be granted peculiar consideration by his more fortunate brethren, to be allowed the privilege of gleaning in the fields, to be given alms, and to be cared for in other ways implicit in the term "brotherhood." A verse like Prov. 19:17 is suggestive of the Lord's care for these unfortunates:

> " He that hath pity upon the poor lendeth unto Yahweh,
> And his good deed will he pay him again."

The original motivation of this attitude was the desire to implement the Biblical category of " community " under the terms of the covenant. The " poor " shared the privileges which the covenant involved and special provision must be made to enable them to sense this fact. In this circumstance, as Rabbi Kohler has observed, " Charity is not a gift of condescending love, but a duty," [4] and the Mishnaic saying becomes intelligible, " If a man will not suffer the poor to glean or suffers one and not another, or aids one of them, he is a robber of the poor " (M. Peah 5:6). There must be no favoritism, for God plays no favorites and in the eyes of the Almighty the poor are all alike, for all are alike needy.

But with the increase of wealth in Israel and its attendant profligacy, the term " poor " took on a new and deeper meaning. This development began long before the exile, but its final issue became apparent only in the post-exilic psalms (e.g., Ps. 34:6), in Deutero-Isaiah, and in Jeremiah, where the word is the practical synonym of " holy " (qadosh), " pious " (hasid), and " godly " (sadiq), and equivalent to the " I " of the Psalter, the typical devout Israelite.

The change in the connotation of the word forms a sad commentary on the degeneracy of the times: the old socio-national basis of the covenant relation in Israel had broken down. Still there was also advance here, for religious experience now took on a hitherto unknown individualization (cf. Ezek. 18:2) and in the new situation the " poor man " attained a new and more truly religious status. He became known as one who sensed, on the one hand, his dire need and, on the other, the fact that this need could be met only on the spiritual plane and through the attainment of a right relation with God. That is to say, in the emergency which faced the " poor man " in the breakdown of the covenant community with its attendant privileges under the law, a sense of spiritual poverty came to match that of physical or material want which had always been his lot.

Such was the character, then, of the "poor man" in the thinking of those addressed by our Lord. His consciousness of "spiritual poverty" constituted his claim to the blessings promised in the next clause (Allen).[5] What these are, it is difficult to define. They are summarized in the phrase "Kingdom of Heaven" (Matthew; "Kingdom of God" in Mark and Luke), which must get its final definition from a painstaking analysis of every passage in the Gospels in which it is used. However, here it must stand for some sort of present reality for the "poor man"; otherwise it would fail to contribute to his desired spiritual growth.

At first the "Kingdom" may mean for him no more than the vision of a *somewhat* that promises to fill up the aching void of his spiritual emptiness. But it must mean at least that to him in actual, present experience, or else God's boon will prove at its very first stage a hollow mockery. And it seems certain in any case that moral or spiritual poverty can be sensed only in contrast to some perception, however inadequate, of its opposite.

In this embryonic sense, therefore, our Lord no doubt thought of the Kingdom of God as a present reality available for every man who sensed his inadequacy and spiritual immaturity. This twofold realization of one's emptiness, on the one hand, and of the Kingdom's fullness, on the other, is the point in the parable of the prodigal son, when of the prodigal's first step in the direction of moral regeneration it is said, "But *when he came to himself* he said, 'How many of my father's hired servants have bread enough and to spare, and I perish here with hunger!'" (Luke 15:17 — "L"). In the parable of the Pharisee and the publican, the publican furnishes us with a like illustration of a spirit aware of its deep unworthiness (Luke 18:13).

Beatitude Two. Repentance

> "God's grace for you penitent —
> you shall find forgiveness!"
>
> (Matt. 5:4.)

The keynote of the second Beatitude is "repentance." The "mourners" here are the repentant in the Hebrew prophet's terminology, those who are troubled at the sinful state of the covenant people. They see clearly that it is sin "which checks and thwarts God's purposes for his people, and delays the coming of the Kingdom" (Allen).[6]

This becomes clear from a comparison of this Beatitude with such passages as Isa. 57:18; 61:1 ff.; etc. Here with the coming salvation in view, which the Lord holds out for his repentant people, he says:

> "I have seen his ways, but I will heal him; I will lead him and requite him with *comfort*, creating for his *mourners* the fruit of the lips."
>
> (Isa. 57:18, italics mine.)

Mourning with fasting constituted in Israel the sign of true repentance, or turning (*shubh*) to God. It was not, it is true, to be taken as a substitute for repentance and so could not be equated with the latter in an absolute sense, but the association of the two ideas was such that the one could be taken as the symbol of the other. Similarly, the "comfort" acquired through God's saving purpose as elaborated by the Second Isaiah would be the assurance of forgiveness granted by God to a sinful people.

The meaning of the second Beatitude, then, is that repentance on man's part will result in forgiveness on God's. Such has been the teaching of Judaism throughout its history, as may be seen in such a passage as Joel 2:12 f.: "'Yet even now,' says the Lord, 'return to me with all your heart, with fasting, with weeping, and with mourning; and rend your hearts and not your garments.' Return to the Lord, your God, for he is gracious and merciful, slow to anger, and abounding in steadfast love, and repents of evil." The same thought is implicit in the famous saying from M. Yoma 8:8: "Repentance effects atonement for lesser transgressions against both positive and negative commands in the law; while for graver transgressions it suspends punishment until the Day of Atonement comes and effects atonement."

Beatitude Three. Trust

" God's blessing on you serene —
    you shall possess the land! "

(Matt. 5:5.)

The keynote of the third Beatitude is " trust." Here the Greek (*praeis*) is variously rendered " meek," " humble-minded," and the like by the translators. But Ps. 37 as a whole, from whose eleventh verse the Beatitude is derived, serves to define the character in question. He is the man who in spite of adversity clings to his faith in the goodness and care of God for the righteous. Through thick and thin his trust is in Yahweh and thus he attains to the settled character of spiritual poise or serenity. The psalmist appears to transfer to such a one his own " unshakable trust in divine providence " and his belief that " they who trust in Yahweh will enjoy permanent peace and quietude." [7] The type of character that is here in question is that which we usually designate as " serenity." Hence the paraphrase, " God's blessing on you serene."

It seems obvious that in the Beatitude the " land " of the psalm is to be understood in a metaphorical sense. There we read at v. 3, " Trust in the Lord, and do good; so you will dwell in the land, and enjoy security." Similarly, in v. 11 the psalmist chants, " But the meek shall possess the land, and delight themselves in abundant prosperity." The psalmist intended, no doubt, that those who in adversity trusted in God would find that eventually the land of their forefathers would be restored to them. But in the Beatitude " land " will be the equivalent of the " Kingdom of God," and the promise will be essentially the same as that found in the first Beatitude. It has often been remarked, moreover, that both in form and in eventual meaning (in the Hebrew), the " poor " man (*'ani*) of the first Beatitude and the " meek " man (*'anaw*) of the third approximate each other. Indeed in the Hebrew the difference between the final letters " yodh " and " waw " in the two words involved amounts about to a fly speck or the slight turn of the pen! It is scarcely surprising, therefore, that in Hebrew manuscripts wherever the word *'ani* appears, some manuscript will have *'anaw* and vice versa.[8]

In the mind of the Evangelist, however, there was no doubt real progress of thought from the first Beatitude to the third. This progress is a sort of spiritual necessity which moves from an initial awareness of one's need to the settled attitude of trust in God alone. The meaning of the third Beatitude, then, will be that the Kingdom is acquired or arrived at in the end and in its richness and fullness only by those who exercise the trust in God needed to receive it. " Whosoever shall not receive the Kingdom of God as a little child, he shall in no wise enter therein " (Mark 10:15) — such is the essence of its teaching.

Beatitude Four. Salvation

" God's boon to you hungry and thirsty for righteousness — you shall find satisfaction! "

(Matt. 5:6.)

The keynote of the fourth Beatitude is " righteousness " or " salvation." Craving for spiritual satisfaction was often expressed in the Old Testament under the imagery of " hunger " and " thirst."

" Ho, every one that thirsteth, come ye to the waters, and he that hath no money; come ye, buy, and eat; yea, come, buy wine and milk without money and without price."

(Isa. 55:1.)

" My soul thirsteth for God, for the living God."

(Ps. 42:2.)

" My soul thirsteth for thee, my flesh longeth for thee in a dry and weary land, where no water is."

(Ps. 63:1.)

It is significant that the satisfaction craved is here expressed in terms of " righteousness," as this fact enables us to locate with a considerable degree of certainty the source material that forms the background of this Beatitude. This is to be found in a series of passages of the Deutero-Isaiah, wherein the imagery is expressive of the salvation God is about to afford his people. The word used by the prophet to define such " salvation " is " righteousness," a term difficult of exact definition and one whose meaning changes with the writer's moods and the particular aspect of salvation which he has in mind at the moment, but expressive certainly both of the character of Yahweh and of that which Israel is to receive from him as a gift of his grace. In the latter sense " righteousness " includes at any rate, as Skinner observes, " the blessings conferred on Israel in token that its right is acknowledged and declared by God." [9]

The equation of the two terms, as we have already seen, is brought out in a number of passages by means of the Hebrew method of synonymous parallelism, thus

> " But my salvation shall be forever,
> And my righteousness shall not be abolished."
> > (Isa. 51:6; see also vs. 5 and 8.)

Salvation, then, in terms of a " righteousness " in the sight of God which confers certain spiritual blessings as well as temporal or material ones upon the people of God, is the final boon afforded in the " Q " series of Beatitudes as adopted and arranged by " Matthew."

From the above study it appears that in stanza one of the Beatitudes it is intended that we observe the moral or spiritual progress of a single individual adjudged as representative of the " sons of the Kingdom." The stages of that progress are, successively, first, an awakening to one's state of inadequacy and moral poverty in the light of the gospel of the Kingdom (Matt. 4:23), however imperfectly this gospel be understood at first; secondly, the determination to " turn " to God in repentance, accompanied by the assurance of the divine forgiveness; thirdly, the adoption of a constant attitude of trust in God alone, to-

gether with a sense of progressive achievement in the acquisition of the " land " (Kingdom); and finally, the earnest longing
to acquire the total " righteousness " which constitutes " salvation " for man.

This moral progress is implicit in the Beatitudes themselves
as arranged by " Matthew." The only question that remains is
whether there is elsewhere in Jesus' teaching any evidence to
support the view that he taught after this fashion. The nearest
parallel, point for point, is perhaps to be found in the parable of
the prodigal son, wherein the boy's moral development is portrayed from " realization " of his state (" he came to himself "),
to " repentance " (" I will arise and go to my father "), thence
to " trust " (" I am no longer worthy to be called your son;
treat me as one of your hired servants "), and finally to " vindi-
cation," or " justification," i.e., " righteousness " in one of its
Isaianic aspects (" But while he was yet at a distance, his father
saw him and had compassion, and ran and embraced him and
kissed him ") (Luke 15:17–24). That Jesus taught the various
elements of this progression in one form and another is too well
known and authenticated to require further demonstration. He
took the entire series of ideas, of course, from the prophetic writings of the Old Testament where they abound in profusion.

Further, that the successive experiences referred to in this
first stanza have significance only if they are carried through to
fruition on the historical plane is from the standpoint of both
psychology and Biblical doctrine generally so clearly patent as to
require no proof. One does not hunger for God's " righteousness " until one has learned to put one's faith in his essential
goodness, nor manifest such trust in him before one has
" turned " toward God in " repentance," nor turn toward him
unless one has realized one's own unworthiness. Moreover, it
seems equally clear that here is no " interims Ethik " applicable
to a limited period under ideal conditions, but rather a normal
series of reactions on the part of men to situations arising in a
very imperfect world and likely to prove normative for such
situations as long as time lasts.[10]

CHAPTER II

Portrait of a Christian — The Image of God

Blessing for those who show mercy —
they shall receive mercy!

Privilege of those who are sincere at heart —
they shall be ushered into God's Presence!

Honor to those who bring peace —
they shall be named " God's sons "!

God's boon to those who are persecuted for their righteousness —
the Kingdom of God is for them!

(Matt. 5:7–10.)

When we turn to the second stanza of the Beatitudes we find ourselves in an entirely different atmosphere. The positive note displaces the negative one, and where before there had been apparent a feeling of emptiness, of an aching void seeking to be filled, here is portrayed the richness of a personality capable of making a vital contribution to the life and uplift of mankind. This second (" M ") series of Beatitudes is the exposition of the " righteousness " or " salvation " mentioned in the last of the other (" Q ") series.

An observation that greatly helps forward both the interpretation of the second stanza and the solution of the literary problems which it presents is the simple one — overlooked by all the commentators apparently — that its structure and content are derived *in toto* from Ps. 85:10:

> " Mercy and truth are met together;
> Righteousness and peace have kissed each other."
>
> (ASV.)

This contention is proved by the undoubted identity of three of
the items chosen for discussion in the two passages of psalm
and Beatitudes — viz., mercy, peace, and righteousness. True,
the Beatitude substitutes " cleansed at heart " (*katharoi te
kardia*) for " truth " of the psalm (in the Hebr. *'emeth*). This,
however, is strictly in line with what one might expect from the
Hebraic coloring of the stanza.

In the Hebrew tradition " truth " was of the essence of God's
person and could be predicated of man only in a secondary or
derived sense. Thus, Sir Edwyn Hoskyns remarks, " The Hebrew mind, in its certainty of a transcendent God, fixed upon
Him as the standard of truth . . . the truth of Jehovah was
regarded as an integral part of His character." [1] G. F. Moore
observes further that for Judaism, " truth (*'emeth*) is the seal of
God," [2] an idea derived from the wording of Dan. 10:21 and
elaborated in the Talmud. The quotation from Daniel reads,
" But I will tell you what is inscribed in the book of truth."
Moore continues: " Since a seal usually bore the name of its
owner, invention was exercised to find a name of God in this
inscription. One took the letters as ' shorthand,' interpreted as
the initials of three words Elohim Melek Tamid, ' Living God
and eternal king ' " (so Jer. 10:10). Professor Moore's meaning
will be immediately clear if we recall that in Hebrew the consonants represent the principal element in the writing. Accordingly, the word *'emeth* in Hebrew is written with the consonant
aleph, which with its vowel will be indicated in English as *'E*,
mim as *M*, and *tau* as *T*. These then successively stand, as Professor Moore has indicated, for the initials in Hebrew of the
three words *Elohim, Melek,* and *Tamid,* which may be interpreted as he has indicated.

Accordingly, it should not strike us as strange that in the Old
Testament in no single instance is " *'emeth* " (" truth," either
noun or adjective) ever predicated of man.[3] The same is true for

the New Testament, a fact which serves to illuminate the stress on truth as found in Jesus which is made in the Johannine literature. Paul's rejoinder to his Jewish critics in Rom. 3:4, "God forbid: yea, let God be found true, but every man a liar," is an *argumentum ad hominem* directed to those of his readers who were acquainted with this Hebrew-Jewish background which would certainly have silenced his opponents at this point and may be taken adequately to represent the views of both Testaments.

Because of these facts it became necessary to adopt some other term for "true" and "truth" so far as these concerned man, one that would suggest a derived character. This was done in the Old Testament in several ways: (*a*) by substituting another word for *'emeth* as employed for God when it was man's truth that was under consideration, both stems meaning, it is true, practically the same thing, but distinguished in this usage (Gen. 42:11, 19, 31, 33 f.); or (*b*) by the adoption of some word or phrase that would supply somewhat the same sense of derived "truth" or "sincerity" [4] (Ps. 24:4; 73:1; Prov. 20:9).

In the present passage, therefore, one or other of these methods undoubtedly lies behind the Greek (*katharoi te kardia*), most likely *bar lebab* in the Hebrew, which may be rendered in the English "a pure heart," the phrase that actually occurs, for example, at Ps. 24:4. And the suggestion that Ps. 85:10 is the source of the "M" stanza of the Beatitudes appears to be as nearly demonstrated as the nature of the case will allow. If we bear this explanation of the Jewish attitude toward the problem of "truth" in mind, therefore, it should be clear that both in our Lord's Beatitudes and in Ps. 85:10 we are dealing with the four attributes of "mercy," "truth," "peace," and "righteousness," or as the RSV at Ps. 85:10 rewords the series for us: "steadfast love," "faithfulness," "righteousness," and "peace." It is perhaps unfortunate that the Old and New Testament translators of the RSV did not get together better than they have done at parallel passages such as the two that are now before us. However, as I have remarked above, the commentators

have apparently failed to notice the connection between the
two passages, so the revisers are hardly to blame!

Briggs makes the illuminating observation that whereas
" truth " and " mercy " were constantly united in the psalms
(cf. Ps. 25:10; 40:10 f.; 57:3; 61:7; 115:1; 138:2), " peace " and
" righteousness " were only so associated here in the Old Testament, as " justice " usually pairs off with " righteousness "
there.[5] The repetition of this combination in the Beatitudes,
therefore, is the more striking and suggests that we are on right
lines in finding the prototype of our second stanza in the psalm
before us.

It becomes relevant, then, to inquire of the teaching of Ps. 85
and particularly of its tenth verse.[6] The psalm divides itself into
two parts, of which the first (vs. 1–7) constitutes the psalmist's
prayer for the " salvation " (yesha') of his people. This prayer
begins at the first verse, " Lord, thou wast favorable to thy
land," and ends with the seventh verse, " Show us thy steadfast
love, O Lord, and grant us thy salvation." The second part
(vs. 8–13), then, is a prophetic oracle introduced by the words,
" Let me hear what God the Lord will speak " (v. 8). These
words recall to us the fact that the function of the prophet in
the first instance was to listen and hear what God had to say to
man. It is evident, therefore, that uttering in his prayer the word
" salvation," the psalmist turns prophet in order to hear God's
definition of salvation. And the significant point for our purpose is that the definition of " salvation " that God is represented as giving is made up of the four terms of our Beatitudes.

The teaching of Ps. 85:10 against this background, then, is
that in the coming or Messianic age the four personified attributes of Yahweh mentioned will meet together to make their
several contributions to a restored and renovated earth. Each
will afford what it has to give for the betterment or salvation of
mankind. As all these attributes belong to God or inhere in
him, it lies on the surface of such teaching that the salvation
which they bring comes as a gift of his grace.

Turning back, now, to the Beatitudes in the light of this

study of the psalm, we shall content ourselves with making several observations which appear to be relevant: First, it appears obvious now that the second stanza of the Beatitudes must be taken as a unit and either attributed to our Lord, or, contrariwise, to the Evangelist, *in toto!* And there appears to be no good reason why Jesus may not have originated the four as they stand in the " M " tradition. It is true that the eighth (v. 10) at first blush appears to be a mere doublet of the ninth (vs. 11 f. from " Q "), but it is not impossible that Jesus uttered it both ways (in both " Q " and " M " forms). It is true, too, that outside of " M " and the single passage in John 16:8–10, Jesus is not reported to have used the word " righteousness " in his teachings. This, however, is surely a mere incident of the tradition and without significance. Its occurrence in Ps. 85:10 would sufficiently account for his singular use of it here. Moreover, our Lord's use of the other attributes mentioned in the verse is too well authenticated to require demonstration.[7]

Secondly, it is most striking that attributes which in the psalm belong to God should here be transferred to man! This can be accounted for only on the assumption that the stanza was uttered in some such " salvation " context as that provided in stanza one. Man's goodness is always represented in Scripture as the mere reflection or image of God's. It is everywhere secondary and derived and the product of a " salvation " which is a gift of God's grace. The assumption underlying this stanza is, therefore, that the " salvation " provided by the Messianic age, or in the eschatological time as envisaged in the psalm, has arrived by the time that these Beatitudes find their fulfillment in man's experience. They are the attributes of men living in and partaking of the grace provided by God in that coming age.

But, thirdly, it seems equally obvious that they are attributes that are required in an imperfect world which itself knows nothing of the blessings of the Messianic " salvation." For where is " mercy " needed save in an age of ruthlessness? Where do men require to learn " sincerity " of motivation except where faithlessness is the rule of the day? Do men bring " peace " except in a world where there is no peace? And who is persecuted for his "righteousness" in a perfect world and under ideal conditions?

It seems, then, that our Lord is sketching a saved personality forced to live in an unsaved world, righteousness surrounded by vice, with the consequent tensions thus created. The Kingdom of God has come for those who are being saved, but for those who are not it is afar off! God's people are living the Kingdom life in an imperfect world; they are, to use Karl Barth's expressive phrase, *"zwischen den Zeiten"* (between time and eternity, living an eternal life in the temporal scene).

Fourthly, the eschatology conceived in this second stanza, as in the first, is prophetic rather than of an apocalyptic type. This had already been noted by commentators to be true of the psalm in question.[8] Both psalmist and the author of the Beatitudes conceived of a renovated earth in which dwells righteousness, not of one removed and apart from our world.[9]

Finally, the elements of this prophetic eschatology, that is, of the Kingdom in its temporal manifestation — in the order of the second stanza's Beatitudes but stated in modern terminology — will be:

Beatitude One —

> " Blessing for those who show mercy —
> they shall receive mercy! "
>
> (Matt. 5:7)

— *a social ethic* of which " mercy " like to God's is the ruling principle and without which men have no right to expect God's mercy to apply to them, a thought entirely in line with our Lord's teaching elsewhere (cf. Mark 11:25).

Beatitude Two —

> " Privilege of those who are sincere at heart —
> they shall be ushered into God's Presence! "
>
> (Matt. 5:8)

— *true religion* on the part of a purified people who, like the
" pure in heart " of Ps. 24:4 are worthy to enter into the temple
of God and to enjoy his fellowship.

Beatitude Three —

> " Honor to those who bring peace —
>   they shall be named ' God's sons '! "

(Matt. 5:9)

— *evangelism*, or the making of peace through the gospel of
peace between those afar off and those who are nigh and of both
with God (Isa. 52:7; 57:18–21; cf. Eph. 2:13 ff.).

Beatitude Four —

> " God's boon to those who are persecuted for their righteous-
>   ness —
>   the Kingdom of God is for them! "

(Matt. 5:10)

— the acquisition of that righteousness which is the true image
of God and which is at once *salvation* for man and his chief end.
Here surely is a program that has relevance for our imperfect
world and one that is calculated to challenge us to well-rounded
Christian living on a very high plane.

A careful exposition of these four Beatitudes in the second
stanza is not called for at this time as the remainder of the
Sermon on the Mount, in Matthew's version at any rate, constitutes our Lord's own interpretation of each of the Beatitudes
of this stanza in turn. Thus, as we shall see, Matt. 5:21–48 is
Jesus' exposition and interpretation of the Beatitude dealing
with social ethics. Similarly the entire content of ch. 6 is taken
up with Jesus' presentation of true religion. And ch. 7 deals
extensively with the acquisition of that righteousness which constitutes salvation for man and is the proper theme of evangelism.

CHAPTER III

Out in Front — The Christian in the World

Yours are these blessings,
    When — with lying intent — men revile you, plague you, speak
        every sort of evil of you on my account.
    Be glad! Exult!
    This is greatly to your benefit in the spiritual realm;
    So, indeed, they plagued the prophets before your time.

You are as " salt to the land "!
    But if salt becomes saltless,
    How will its saltness be restored?
    It is then fit for naught
    But is cast out to be trampled by men.

You are as " light to the world "!
    No city lying perched upon a hill can be concealed:
    No lamp do men light and place beneath a peck measure;
    Rather, they put it on a lampstand —
    Then it sheds its light for all those at home.
Let your light so shine out in men's view
That they may observe your " good works "
And give the praise to your Father
Who dwells in the spiritual realm.

                          (Matt. 5:11–16.)

This short passage, as it stands in Matthew's Gospel at any
rate, rather clearly represents the application of the Beatitude
poem to Jesus' immediate disciples. It is made up, as the print-
ing shows, of three short paragraphs cast in poetic mold. The
poetic structure here, however, is somewhat more complicated

than that occurring in the Beatitudes. Possibly Matthew found
it difficult to translate the underlying Aramaic into a Greek
dress and in so doing in large part succeeded in obscuring the
original poetic structure. Comparison with the co-ordinate passage in Luke 6:22 suggests that Matthew even went so far as
to make certain changes of his own, though it always remains
possible that these had been made in the source of the sermon
which came into his hands.[1]

It is a rather commonly accepted theory among New Testament scholars that v. 10 in Matthew is a repetition of Luke's
fourth Beatitude (Luke 6:22 — " Q "). This suggestion is made
because in vs. 10 and 11, Matthew mentions persecution, and
so it is suggested that Matthew has derived his v. 10 from the
" Q " source which he has in common with Luke and v. 11
from his own source " M." It is to be noted, however, that the
verb " to plague " or " to persecute " (found in both verses in
Matthew) does not occur in Luke's version of the Beatitude.
Moreover, as we have already seen in Chapter II above, Matthew's v. 10 forms an integral part of our Lord's interpretation
of Ps. 85:10. It is much more likely, therefore, that stanza two
of the Beatitudes, discussed in Chapter II, forms a unit in itself
and that Matthew's employing the verb translated " to persecute " or as here " to plague " in v. 11 is derived from our Lord's
use of the verb as Matthew transmits it in v. 10.

At all events, the first paragraph of the application of the
Beatitudes stresses for Jesus' disciples the necessity of their
vicarious suffering for the sake of the Kingdom.

" Yours are these blessings,
    When — with lying intent — men revile you, plague you,
        speak every sort of evil of you on my account.
    Be glad! Exult!
    This is greatly to your benefit in the spiritual realm;
    So, indeed, they plagued the prophets before your time."
                                              (Matt. 5:11 f.)

The object is to comfort the disciples by bringing the thought
of their suffering for Jesus (" on my account ") into conjunc-

tion with the sufferings of the prophets of all times. Jesus shows
no intention of minimizing the necessity of his disciples' suffering for the sake of the Kingdom. The teaching here is rather in
line with that found in the other sources of his teachings in
the Gospels, for example, at Luke 14:27: "Whoever does not
take up his cross and follow after me, cannot be my disciple,"
and Matt. 10:37 f.: "He who loves father or mother more than
me is not worthy of me; and he who loves son or daughter more
than me is not worthy of me; and he who does not take his
cross and follow me is not worthy of me."

The same note is struck in our Lord's conversation with
James and John in connection with their request to sit at the
right and the left hand of his throne in his Kingdom (Mark 10:
35–45). In reply Jesus asked them, "Are you able to drink the
cup which I am drinking, or to be baptized with the baptism
with which I am being baptized?" Similarly, when men came
to Jesus professing their willingness to follow him, he made
every endeavor to state clearly the conditions of such following
and to dissuade them if they were not prepared to undertake
the fulfillment of such conditions. Luke contains a series of short
parabolic sayings calculated to dissuade anyone from following
him who does not first "count the cost" (Luke 14:28–33).

And our Lord on this occasion concluded this series with the
express statement, "So, therefore, whoever of you does not re-
nounce all that he has cannot be my disciple" (v. 33). Similarly, both Matthew (ch. 8:18–22) and Luke (ch. 9:57–62)
contain a series of warnings to the overglib who would follow
Jesus without reckoning the cost of doing so. To such, Jesus
replies, "Foxes have holes, the birds of the air have nests; but
the Son of Man has nowhere to lay his head." In all such passages Jesus makes it plain that following him and the demands
of the Kingdom must take precedence over all human relation-
ships and demands. The sum of the matter is well stated in
Luke 9:62: "No one who puts his hand to the plow and looks
back is fit for the Kingdom of God."

The evidence then appears to be overwhelming that the note

of vicarious suffering for the sake of the Kingdom held a large place in the teaching of Jesus to his disciples throughout his ministry. It need not be doubted that this formed one of the themes of his teaching from the earliest part of his ministry, as the presence of it in this application of the Beatitudes to the condition of his immediate disciples would suggest. The thought of vicarious suffering does not appear in Ps. 85, from which stanza two of the Beatitudes is taken. It is present, however, in Deutero-Isaiah, particularly in the Suffering Servant songs, from which, as we have seen, portions of stanza one were drawn.

There is every likelihood, therefore, that our Lord throughout his ministry thought of, not only himself, but also his disciples as sharing in the Suffering Servant concept.[2] "Taking up the cross," "drinking the cup," "being baptized with his baptism" — all these expressions were to mean for Jesus' disciples that they, like him, were to have a share in the bringing in of the Kingdom of God through vicarious suffering. The great Deutero-Isaiah, in the history of religious thought, was possibly the first to discern the fact that only so could God's redemptive purpose for man be fulfilled.[3] The later leadership of the church of the New Testament, and particularly our Lord's greatest disciple, the apostle Paul, clearly discerned the necessity of such suffering if God's purpose for man was to be fulfilled. Listen to Paul, for example, as he writes to the church at Colossae: "Now I rejoice in my sufferings for your sake, and in my flesh I complete what is lacking in Christ's afflictions for the sake of his body, that is, the church" (Col. 1:24). There is a type of pseudo piety in the Christian church today which decries any comparison of one's sufferings with those of Christ. But neither Jesus himself nor his apostle Paul took alarm at such comparison. As the above quotations make abundantly evident, both held strenuously to the maxim, "Like master, like man." That Jesus called his disciples of all ages to share in his redemptive sufferings there can be no doubt, and the type of pseudo piety to which reference has just been made can have no other effect than a disastrous one upon the evangelistic activity of the church!

Some years ago one of my students in the seminary remarked, " My classmates and I have been here now for approximately a year and a half and as a result of the teaching in this seminary many of us have just about lost our faith." He proceeded to ask me what I would do about it! My reply was along these lines: " I would suggest that you go to your room and drop upon your knees and thank God that you have been thought worthy to enter this institution with a view to losing your faith and regaining it at a deeper level." I went on to ask him whether he did not realize that he was to preach the gospel to a world that had lost its faith, and I inquired whether he thought that were possible if he had not gone through a like experience of loss of faith himself and issued victoriously from it!

Incidentally, I suggested that while upon his knees he should endeavor to experience the joy which one may have in the midst of such vicarious suffering, realizing that it was vicarious and had redemptive value. And it is this note that is struck next in this very short paragraph of our Lord's teaching: " Be glad! Exult! This is greatly to your benefit in the spiritual realm; so, indeed, they plagued the prophets before your time." It is not to be thought that there is anything morbid in the teaching of our Lord at this point. Neither here nor elsewhere does he ever suggest that suffering is of any worth whatever for its own sake. Nor does he ever, like Bishop Ignatius of Syrian Antioch, gloat over the necessity for his own suffering or that of his disciples. In his Epistle to the Romans, Ignatius pleaded with his readers not to endeavor to spare him from the arena and the privilege which he foresaw of being thrown to the lions! [4] Nothing of this morbid attitude toward martyrdom ever appears in our Lord's teaching.

However, it is beyond question that our Lord experienced the " benefit " referred to for himself and taught that his disciples would with him experience the joy of vicarious suffering. His cry, " It is finished," reported in John's Gospel (ch. 19:30) is one of victory experienced in the midst of apparent defeat on the cross. The above quotation from the apostle Paul indicates that he also experienced this joy in the midst of the agony attending vicarious suffering. And the strong feeling of exultation on the part of this great disciple of Jesus Christ is unmistakable when he writes words like the following: " Five times I have received at the hands of the Jews the forty lashes less one. Three times I have been beaten with rods; once I was stoned. Three times I have been shipwrecked; a night and a day I have been adrift at sea; on frequent journeys, in danger from rivers, danger from robbers, danger from my own people, danger from Gentiles, danger in the city, danger in the wilderness, danger at sea, danger from false brethren; in toil and hardship," and the like (II Cor. 11:24–27).

One gains the impression that the apostle Paul would have imagined something to be very wrong were a month to go by without a shipwreck or his being beaten with rods or stoned! And yet there is nothing morbid in such teaching on our Lord's part or that of his great apostle. The joy derived from such suffering finds its *raison d'être* in the goal that is had in view and the sense that through suffering it is to be accomplished, and only so.

Our Lord's reference to the prophets in the passage was with a view to establishing this point. The sufferings of the prophets came to them, as was well known, because they were messengers of the Word of God to man and because man in his desperation is always unwilling to receive that Word with equanimity. Our Lord made this the subject of his parable of the unfaithful husbandmen (Mark 12:1–11). The servants in that parable who came to the husbandmen seeking " some of the fruit of the vineyard " for its owner were beaten, cast out, and killed because they were under orders from the vineyard's owner. Such were the prophets, and their orders — enshrined in the Word of God to them — made them a part of the redemptive process.

No doubt the secular world is unable to discern how vicarious

suffering can be of "benefit in the spiritual realm" to those
who experience it. But that such is the case is a commonplace
of Christian experience. The service of the Kingdom, of the
gospel, of the Lord Christ himself — these bring their reward in
joy and that "peace that passeth understanding" which the
world cannot know nor receive.

The fact should not escape our attention that the persecution, which in v. 10 is said to arise because of "righteousness,"
in v. 11 is experienced on Jesus' account. As T. W. Manson has
pointed out, the demands of Jesus on his followers are sharply
revised immediately following Peter's achievement of the insight that Jesus was indeed the Messiah. "In the Marcan account, the pregnant phrase 'for my sake' now first makes its
appearance: and the things that must be borne 'for my sake'
are the loss of property, friends, relatives, personal liberty, and
even life itself." [5]

In the Lucan account of this paragraph (Luke 6:22-23) there
are two Aramaic expressions lying behind the Greek which
point up the fact that this is indeed Aramaic poetry on our
Lord's part. The first of these — translated in the RSV "cast
out your name as evil" — probably should read, as the Aramaic
behind the Greek undoubtedly means, "publish against you an
evil name." Similarly, the phrase "leap for joy," as Matthew
Black has recently pointed out, no doubt has behind it the
Aramaic word *dus*, a word "associated with movement and
dancing." [6]

As the first of the three paragraphs under discussion in this
chapter represents the application of the Beatitudes to Jesus'
disciples in the "Q" sermon, so paragraphs two and three represent the application of the second stanza of the Beatitudes
more especially to the same disciples in the "M" sermon. We
have already seen that in this second stanza occurs an analysis
of the meaning of salvation for man in terms of Ps. 85:10. That
analysis involves the attainment of the likeness of God and the
consequent reflection of the divine attributes of "mercy" and
"truth," "righteousness" and "peace" in the characters and

personalities of men. Our Lord now suggests that such men — namely, the " sons of the Kingdom," his understanding disciples — are the " salt " and " light " of the body of mankind at large.

> " You are as ' salt to the land '!
> But if salt becomes saltless,
> How will its saltness be restored?
> It is then fit for naught
> But is cast out to be trampled by men."
>
> (Matt. 5:13.)

This paragraph begins with what may very well embody an aphoristic saying common in Jesus' day: " You are as ' salt to the land '! " If, however, such a saying ever existed, it has not been discovered by modern scholars, and it is far more likely that Jesus is the author of the aphorism himself.[7]

What is more important is to inquire regarding the nature of this " saltness " which the true son of the Kingdom possesses; and at this point there has been much speculation. Some have suggested that our Lord had in mind the preservative function of salt, or, again, its seasoning quality, and the like. It is probable, however, that the key to this problem is to be found in the parallel verse at Luke 14:35. Here Matthew Black translates, " It [i.e., salt which has become saltless] is neither fit for the ground, nor yet for dung." [8] The Aramaic lying behind the Greek words meaning " for the ground " and " for dung," respectively, would be *leʾarʿa* and *lerēʿa*. The play on words is obvious here to anyone who will pronounce them. This, then, is an example of Semitic parallelism of expression, and the equivalent phrases — " for the ground " and " for dung " — would mean the same or approximately the same thing. In other words, it is the fertilizing or life-giving quality of salt that is had in mind, and our Lord means to say that his disciples, the " sons of the Kingdom," are life-givers among men. They possess within themselves a fructifying or generating power which mankind generally does not possess.

What, then, is this thing in his disciples which Jesus speaks

of as " saltness "? In the light of the over-all context of the
sermon and particularly of the preceding vs. 6 and 10, it can
be no other than the " righteousness " of the gospel which lies
at the very heart of the disciples' experience of the Kingdom.
As we have already seen, this righteousness stands in the first
instance for the redemptive character of God, and it is because
of his grace that Jesus' disciples share that character, that they
have life-giving power for mankind generally.

> " You are as ' light to the world '!
>> No city lying perched upon a hill can be concealed:
>> No lamp do men light and place beneath a peck meas-
>> ure;
>> Rather, they put it on a lampstand —
>> Then it sheds its light for all those at home.
> Let your light so shine out in men's view
> That they may observe your ' good works '
> And give the praise to your Father
> Who dwells in the spiritual realm."
>
>   (Matt. 5:14–16.)

Paragraph three of our passage likewise begins with an aphorism of our Lord: " You are as ' light to the world '! " The like
of this saying is not found elsewhere in the Gospels, and it is
probable that Matthew found it in his special source. The parallelism between the two aphorisms in vs. 13 and 14, however,
would suggest that for Jesus' mind they stand for approximately
the same thing, namely, the life- or light-giving quality of
discipleship. And it is a notable fact that in the thought of the
day, both within Judaism and the surrounding Greek world,
life and light were considered as joined together in an intimate
relationship. A very good example of this thought, of course,
occurs in the Prologue to John's Gospel. When in the Prologue
(ch. 1:4) John says that " in him was life, and the life was the
light of men," he effectively sums up the Old Testament teaching as it is seen, for example, at Ps. 36:9: " For with thee is the
fountain of life; in thy light do we see light." To see light is to
live, light and life being synonymous. (Job 3:16; 33:30.)

It is clear that this equation was also characteristic of contemporary Greek religious and philosophical thought; much of the mythological substructure of the popular religions dealt with the recurring battle of light and life against darkness and death. C. K. Barrett concludes a review of this evidence with the statement: " Even more significant for John than this varied background was the fact that Jesus had, by his miracles, resurrection, and continued power in the supernatural life of the church, proved himself to be the life of the world." [9]

Although the aphorism itself in v. 14 is not found elsewhere in the Gospels, what follows has an approximate parallel at Mark 4:21 f. as follows: " Is a lamp brought in to be put under a bushel, or under a bed, and not on a stand? For there is nothing hid, except to be made manifest; nor is anything secret, except to come to light." This passage from Mark, and vs. 15 and 16 which immediately follow in Matthew, together suggest that " light " denoted for Jesus the evangelizing power resident in discipleship. If the " son of the Kingdom " possessed that character of saltness which stood for the life-giving or fructifying power of the gospel, then (to change the metaphor) he should allow it to manifest itself in the gospel's propagation even as the light shines in a dark world. In other words, the life-giving power at the heart of the gospel is not something the disciple is to hug to himself, to nourish for his own good alone. Rather, that life is to be shared with others and with all the world around.

There is, indeed, in the change of metaphor from " salt " to " light " the suggestion that, if life is indeed present in the disciple, it cannot be other than shared with those whom he contacts in the world. For it is indigenous to life that it gives life to others. As this is a law in the natural world, so it is a law in the spiritual world. " Good works," therefore, are by no means the cause of salvation but rather its fruit. Those who have within themselves the character of saltness or of life produced by the righteous redemptive activity of God in their lives can do no other than to share it in saving activity. It should be obvious then to all the world, as to the disciples themselves, that the praise for such good works goes not to the disciples but to the Father who is himself the life-giving Agent at work within the disciples' lives. (Eph. 2:10.)

Incidentally, the description of the Father as one " who is in heaven," or, as we have translated, " who dwells in the spiritual realm," is not original with Jesus. It was the common description of God characteristic of contemporary and succeeding Judaism.[10]

CHAPTER IV

Kingdom Righteousness

Do not imagine that
   I have come on the scene to nullify law or prophets:
   Not to rescind, rather to implement, have I come.

I tell you truly,
   " Until heaven and earth depart,
   From Scripture shall neither ' yodh ' nor ' qarna ' depart,
   Until all things find fulfillment.
Whoever, then, relaxes one of these ordinances — the least,
   And teaches men so to do,
   ' Least ' shall he be called in God's Kingdom.
Whoever, again, does and teaches them,
   ' Great ' shall he be called in God's Kingdom."

For I tell you,
   " Except your ' righteousness ' excel that of rabbis and Phari-
      sees,
   Never will you enter God's Kingdom."

(Matt. 5:17–20.)

The passage that was under discussion in the last chapter
dealt, it will be recalled, with the application of the Beatitudes
to the circumstances of the immediate followers of Jesus. It
closed with the suggestion that those disciples should not hesi-
tate to allow their " good works " to be seen by men inasmuch
as they represented the will of God for mankind generally.

In the short paragraph before us in the present chapter, Jesus
turns his attention to the will of God for his own life. We are
immediately struck with the fact that he places himself in the
line of God's revelational and redemptive activity through the

ages. He no more stands alone than do his disciples in their experience of persecution and tribulation at the hands of their contemporaries. Those disciples are to share the tribulations experienced by the prophets (vs. 11–12). He stands within the same line and declares accordingly, " I have come on the scene not to nullify law or prophets; not to rescind, rather to implement, have I come."

That our Lord sensed the fact that he was an element — to be sure, by far the most important and concluding element — in the revelational-redemptive line is clear from many of his utterances. Perhaps the most striking of all is his parable of the wicked husbandmen (Mark 12:1–8). It is generally agreed that in this parable the servants whom the lord of the vineyard sends to receive some of the fruit thereof are the prophets of Israel and Judah, and obviously the " son " at the end of this line is our Lord himself.[1]

As in the parable, so here we gain the impression that our Lord is not only at the end of the revelational-redemptive line, but that in a very real sense it has all been specifically and intentionally leading up to him. He is in the prophetic line but greater than a prophet; for only he can be designated " Son." Likewise in the passage before us we have the feeling that he stands alone and aloof, over against both law and prophets which came before him. There is, therefore, both continuity and discontinuity on his part as relates to all those who have gone before.

> " Do not imagine that
> I have come on the scene to nullify law or prophets:
> Not to rescind, rather to implement, have I come."
>   (Matt. 5:17.)

That what we have been saying represents our Lord's true attitude toward the previous revelation of God to his people is evident from the summary words that he uses to describe that revelation, namely, " law " and " prophets." These two terms were often used by the contemporary Judaism of his day to sum

up the entire Old Testament scriptures. At times a third word
— "writings" — was joined with them and intended to include
the psalms and other poetical and wisdom literature. One could,
therefore, speak of the Old Testament as composed of law,
prophets, and writings. But it was also possible to speak of
those scriptures in terms of their two more important parts as
"law and prophets." At times the term "law" alone was used
to describe the whole Old Testament.[2] It is therefore the entire
revelation of God as contained in the Old Testament scriptures
which our Lord has in mind and which on his own declaration
presents to him a challenge — the challenge, namely, of destroying or fulfilling.[3]

But it is quite impossible to conceive of our Lord, born and
raised as he was within the context of Judaism and sensitive to
the fact that God had undoubtedly spoken through the prophets to the fathers before his day, as wishing to "destroy" what
had gone before him. When the Johannine Jesus speaks of
all those before his day as being "thieves and robbers" (John
10:8), as the context clearly indicates, he has in mind, not the
prophets and certainly least of all the last of the prophets —
John the Baptist — but rather those false pretenders to Mes-
siahship who had preceded him. Like Jesus himself, these false
messiahs had made the claim to "have come on the scene"
with a view to taking up the work that the prophets had laid
down. But they had made their claims out of selfish motivation
and not for the sake of the "sheep" of God's sheepfold (John
10:10). Hence they were false shepherds, thieves, robbers, de-
spoilers of the flock.

It was the moral supremacy of Jesus Christ, his unselfish purpose with reference to God's people, that verified his character
as the true Shepherd of God's "sheep." The writers of the New
Testament are unanimous in witnessing to this fact of our
Lord's deep sense of mission, which was unlike that of all who
had gone before him. Matthew's special source alone among
the Gospels defines this sense of mission as one to "fulfill all
righteousness" (Matt. 3:15). This righteousness, as we have

already seen, stands for the whole duty which God requires of man. Jesus alone senses his ability to fulfill this righteous will of God for man. Doubtless it is this same sense on our Lord's part to which the present passage wishes to give expression.[4]

But if he is not to nullify or rescind law or prophets, what then is his function with reference to them? The Greek word that we have translated " to implement " has been variously translated " to fulfill " and " to complete." It is now rather generally agreed, one imagines, that the latter translation is inadequate. It is true, of course, that our Lord did complete the revelation which God had to give to man. It is this factor to which John 1:17 gives expression: " For the law was given through Moses; grace and truth came through Jesus Christ." But in the context of this Sermon's teaching as a whole, it becomes apparent that our Lord is not at the moment thinking of what he may have to add to either law or prophets by way of new revelation.

The translation " to fulfill " is therefore to be preferred. Or, perhaps, as the following chapters would seem to suggest, our Lord has in mind what we intend to convey by the verb " to implement." For, to implement is to realize in experience, to bring into actual operation, to do whatever may be necessary that a principle or policy may actually be carried out. The context of the following teachings suggests that it is this which our Lord has in mind. It is not only that he has some duty to perform relative to the law and prophets. His task is far greater than this. It is rather that he shall lay the groundwork, shall simplify and expound the ethical and religious problems, shall create and nourish a new spirit within his followers, that the requirements of law and prophets together may find implementation in their lives.

> " I tell you truly,
>   ' Until heaven and earth depart,
>   From Scripture shall neither " *yodh* " nor " *quarna* " depart,
>   Until all things find fulfillment.' "

(Matt. 5:18.)

The remainder of this passage is intended to indicate how seriously our Lord meant what he has just said. For him the Scriptures are as durable as God's created universe. In so saying, Jesus was giving expression to a thought acceptable to the Judaism of his day. For an example of such teaching, one may note the passage at Prov. 8:22 where Wisdom (the Law) says of itself: " The Lord created me at the beginning of his work, the first of his acts of old," and again in the rabbinical comment (Sifre) on Deut. 11:10: " The Torah, because it is more highly prized than everything, was created before everything." That is, the law (Torah) is taken to be as much a part of God's activity as creation itself, and hence just as durable.

In giving expression to this thought, our Lord makes use of the smallest letter of the Hebrew alphabet (" yodh "), as well as of a word suggestive of the flourish added to certain letters by the rabbis with a view to ornamenting them (" qarna "). The suggestion is sometimes made that " yodh " stands, therefore, for the least commandment of the Mosaic law, whereas " qarna " represents the pharisaical additions and explanations of the law found in the later codified Mishnah and Talmud. People who hold this view go on to suggest that the saying appears to commit Jesus to an acceptance of the " traditions of the elders," as well as of the Mosaic law itself, and this, it is argued, cannot represent his true position. It is suggested, therefore, that the context of the saying in Luke's Gospel (ch. 16:17) is to be preferred. There Jesus may be interpreted as saying with sharp irony that " it would be easier for heaven and earth to pass away than that his enemies permit one embellishment added by them to the law to fail." If this is our Lord's meaning, then obviously Matthew has misunderstood and misapplied the saying in the present context.

Some who adopt this interpretation of the passage go on to suggest that in vs. 19 and 20 the one called " least " in God's Kingdom is no doubt the apostle Paul. The entire passage, then, becomes a diatribe of the later Jewish Christian community, the " Judaizers " of Galatians, against our Lord's great apostle for

his having relaxed the ordinances of the law in favor of his
teaching on justification by grace alone through faith. In this
case, of course, the saying is supposed to have been read back
into Jesus' mouth by the Jewish church and is unauthentic as
it stands.[5]

This argument, however, as it relates to the apostle Paul appears to be peculiarly inappropriate. There is no evidence that
the apostle desired at any point in his career to relax the least
of the enactments of the law. Quite the contrary, he observed
on more than one occasion that those who were under the law
were bound to keep the law in its entirety. (Rom. 2:17–23;
Gal. 5:3.) If we may judge from Paul's letters — and we have
no other means of making a judgment in the matter — it was
not the fact that he relaxed any of the ordinances of the law
which his opponents held against him. Their complaint rather
seems to have been that he set the law in its entirety aside.
And to this he replied: " Do we then overthrow the law by this
faith? By no means! On the contrary, we uphold the law."
(Rom. 3:31.)

We are at liberty, therefore, to imagine that, as Hans Windisch has suggested, the passage before us represents a condition
of affairs existing in our Lord's own day and long before the
Judaizers had brought their guns to bear on the apostle Paul.[6]
It is quite conceivable that in that early period, before the controversy over the law had taken shape, Jesus felt impelled to
state his position before his enemies with regard to the Old
Testament scriptures. This would seem to have been the more
necessary because of the revolutionary character of his teaching, which took into account, not the laws for their own sake,
but rather the contribution they might make to the acquisition
of a spirit on the part of Jesus' disciples which would in the end
place them above all law. In this early context it is quite conceivable that Jesus should have said, not only that no law or
ordinance should fail from God's revelation, but also that the
scribal embellishments to the same had a function to perform
within the divine will.

In any case it is an oversimplification of the problem and its solution facing Jesus to suggest that he should have chosen to give his allegiance to the law (yodh) rather than to the scribal traditions (qarna). So far as our evidence goes, this was exactly the position of the Sadducees and of the Qumran sect of Jesus' day. But it is certainly clear that Jesus was neither a Sadducee nor an Essene. Mark 7:8 is often quoted in this connection ("You leave the commandment of God, and hold fast the tradition of man"). But it is quite unfair to both Jesus and the Pharisees to interpret the Marcan incident at ch. 7:1–13 as indicative that Jesus was upholding the written Torah and the Pharisees their traditions. The Pharisees were above everything else zealous for the Torah, and their traditions were the product of an earnest wish to put it into practice in daily living. That Jesus knew this is certain. The Sabbath controversies make this plain.

Probably a right understanding of our Lord's attitude in the Marcan passage and elsewhere will be arrived at if we assume that he is presenting an *argumentum ad hominem* to his enemies along the lines of their attack on his disciples. They had accused his disciples of disobeying the law by not washing their hands before meals. He replies in like kind and shows that in obeying their traditions they, too, are actually — though, to be sure, unwittingly — disobeying the very law they were attempting earnestly to uphold and to implement. It was, then, neither law nor traditions as such which our Lord was concerned to preserve or to implement. Rather, he sought to propagate a spirit that could use both to the glory of God and to the service of his Lordship in the world.

> "Whoever, then, relaxes one of these ordinances — the least,
>> And teaches men so to do,
>>> 'Least' shall he be called in God's Kingdom.
>> Whoever, again, does and teaches them,
>>> 'Great' shall he be called in God's Kingdom."
>>>> (Matt. 5:19.)

If, then, Jesus actually uttered the words in v. 18, as the present writer believes he did, the question must of necessity arise: For whom in our Lord's intention do the words "least" and "great" in God's Kingdom stand (v. 19)? And in what sense do the doing and teaching of the laws of the Old Covenant, rather than their relaxation, form a criterion for one's standing in the Kingdom of Heaven?

The first of these questions is perhaps to be answered from the parallel passage in "Q" at Matt. 11:11 and Luke 7:28: "He who is least in the Kingdom of God is greater than he" (that is, than John the Baptist). In this passage the dividing line that marks the coming of the Kingdom of Heaven (or "of God") is that which separates John the Baptist from Jesus. In other words, the Kingdom of Heaven comes with our Lord's appearance and ministry among men. It is now present, and it is in this present Kingdom therefore that men will begin to be called "least" or "great" by reference to their having observed the commandments of the Old Covenant.

The second question involving the employment of the law as a criterion for the judging of the quality of discipleship in the present Kingdom must await fuller explication in the chapters that follow. For the moment it will be sufficient to note that the controversy between Judaism and Christianity, relative to the keeping of the commandments of the law, has pertained, not to the *fact*, but rather to the *method* of and *motivation* for the same. Beginning with its Lord himself, the Christian church has never denied the necessity of the Christian's fulfilling the high ethical and religious demands of the law. It has affirmed, however, that in acquiring a spirit that sets one above the necessity of receiving a divine fiat to do this and not to do that, the Christian is in a far better way than any legalist actually to fulfill the law's demand.

> "For I tell you,
>> 'Except your "righteousness" excel that of rabbis and Pharisees,
>> Never will you enter God's Kingdom.'"
>
> (Matt. 5:20.)

And it would seem that this is exactly the point that our Lord wishes to make in v. 20, by way of introducing a series of

examples taken from the law itself as to how man is to fulfill
the will of God for his life. It is beyond question that the rabbis
and Pharisees, who are to bear the brunt of our Lord's attack
both here and elsewhere in his ministry, were reckoned as the
best examples of moral and spiritual living under the law. It is
startling, accordingly, to read our Lord's words, " Except your
' righteousness' excel that of rabbis and Pharisees, never will
you enter God's Kingdom." Clearly, therefore, in the passages
that follow by way of example of his method of fulfilling the
law's demand, it is not our Lord's will in the very least to lessen
the demands of the law. Rather, it is his wish to sharpen these
and to indicate how very deeply they cut into the pattern of
daily living. With this introduction in which our Lord has
stated his own attitude toward the law and the scriptures of his
people as a whole, we now turn to the examples he sets forth by
way of clarification of the one major principle that he wishes
to teach.[7]

B. KINGDOM RIGHTEOUSNESS AND THE PERSONS OF OTHERS

CHAPTER V

Respecting the Persons of Others

You have received by tradition the saying to men of old,
"Thou shalt not commit murder" — and —
"Whoever murders shall be liable to judgment.'

I say to you, however,
"Everyone who is angry at his brother
Shall be liable to judgment:
Whoever addresses his brother, 'Empty head,'
Shall be liable to the assembly:
Whoever addresses [his brother], 'Heretic,'
Shall be liable to fiery hell."

If, then, you are presenting your offering at the altar
And there are reminded that your brother holds animosity
against you,
Leave your offering there at the altar,
Go, first effect a reconciliation with your brother,
Then, come, present your offering.
Come quickly to terms with your opponent,
While with him on the road,
Lest your opponent drag you before a judge,
The judge commit you to an officer of the court,
The officer throw you into jail.
Truly I tell you,
"You will never get out of there till you have paid out your
last cent!"

(Matt. 5:21–26.)

In one way and another we have thus far been observing that the theme of this Sermon on the Mount is Jesus' understanding of the nature of the "righteousness" or whole duty which God

65

requires of man. Moreover, our Lord has made it clear that there is a peculiar Christian attitude, as distinguished from that of the scribes and Pharisees of the day, relative to the meaning of the term "righteousness" and how man's duty with regard to it is to be fulfilled. With this in mind, the first part of this book has been entitled "Traveling the Christian Way." In our study of the first stanza of the Beatitudes, we observed that Jesus briefly outlined the stages of this Christian Way, closing with the suggestion that the "son of the Kingdom" will hunger and thirst after the Christian pattern of righteousness. Then in stanza two we were given a brief summary of what this righteousness would involve, first in relation to one's fellows and secondly in relation to God.

The second major part of the sermon, which is immediately before us, carries us through Matt. 5:21–48 and obviously deals with one's relation to one's fellow. It is not too much to say, therefore, that this portion of the Sermon is our Lord's own interpretation of Beatitude Five, namely, "Blessing for those who show mercy — they shall receive mercy!" The problem with which he is dealing here is: What does it mean to show mercy to one's fellow men?

A number of years ago in an address to students, Karl Barth remarked that the first word in Christian theology or man's teaching about God is "grace," and that therefore the first word in ethics or the teaching about man's relations with his fellows must be "grace." Certainly this remark by the Swiss theologian is true. It is fundamental to all Biblical teaching that man is made in the "image of God." This can mean nothing less than that God is the "pattern" for all of man's living. As therefore God is holy, righteous, true, just, loving, merciful, gracious, so man must be all these things. And as the very acme of God's relation to man is that one for which the words "grace," "mercy," "love" stand, so must it be with man's relation to his fellow.[1]

With a view, then, in this portion of the Sermon to interpret the meaning of "mercy," Jesus first treats of one's attitude to the entire person of his fellow (vs. 21–26), then of one's attitude to the person of the opposite sex (vs. 27–32), and thereafter analyzes the person of man into the three parts that are generally recognized as constituting that person — viz., the mind (vs. 33–37), the will (vs. 38–42), and the emotions (vs. 43–47).

" You have received by tradition the saying to men of old,
    ' Thou shall not commit murder ' — and —
    ' Whoever murders shall be liable to judgment.' "
(Matt. 5:21.)

In the present chapter, then, we are to see his teaching regarding a man's respect for the persons of others as such. As was the usual scribal fashion in his day, Jesus begins his teaching and founds it upon a quotation from the Old Testament, in this case from Ex. 20:13 and Deut. 5:17, namely, " Thou shalt not commit murder."

But though he begins as do the rabbis in his day with a Scripture quotation, our Lord's motivation in doing so is quite different from theirs. The scribes were concerned, as they said, to " make a hedge about the law " (M. Aboth 1:1). That is to say, they were consciously circumscribed by the letter of the law and never ventured to go beyond it. On the contrary, their one aim was to set forth a series of statutory interpretations of the law in such a way that it might be applied and obeyed in life situations. Many illustrations may be given in support of the contention that their interest first and last was in the " letter of the law," and in an eminent desire to make it workable in a practical fashion. To say, therefore, " it is written " was for them the final argument on any subject. The scribes' " righteousness," accordingly, was made up of an earnest desire to carry out the letter of the law as it stood. Matthew Black has pointed out that the expression " you have heard " was one employed by the rabbis to mean " to receive [traditional] teaching from " a scholar of note. The translation of the oft-recurring clause in our present section of the Sermon — " You have received by tradition the saying to men of old " — is in accordance with Black's suggestion at this point. Occurring as it does as a sort of refrain throughout the passage, it is certainly intended by our Lord as a buffer against his teaching, which begins in each case, " I say to you, however." [2]

Nothing could be clearer in the present section of the Sermon than that to implement the law and the prophets meant for our Lord not the explicit carrying out of the literal statement involved in the ordinances of the law; rather, the implementation involved, to his mind, a going far beyond the simple statement of the law's demands to inquire of the motivation in the mind of the lawgiver — God himself — and of his good intention for man's well-being.

> " I say to you, however,
>   ' Everyone who is angry at his brother
>   Shall be liable to judgment:
>   Whoever addresses his brother, " Empty head,"
>   Shall be liable to the assembly:
>   Whoever addresses [his brother], " Heretic,"
>   Shall be liable to fiery hell.' "
>
> (Matt. 5:22.)

The present instance and its reference to the overt act of murder offers us a good example of the carrying out of this principle. The law quoted dealt only with the overt act, and accordingly the rabbis pronounced that " whoever murders shall be liable to judgment," meaning thereby no doubt in the first instance man's judgment and in the second, God's. But with the law's pronouncement before his hearers, Jesus proposes his own in opposition thereto: " I say to you, however." And then he proceeds to condemn, not the overt act, but rather the inner attitude or motivation from which the act springs, viz., that of anger against one's brother. It is, then, this anger in the heart of a man, and such words as " empty head " and " heretic " which spring from that anger and tend to belittle or impugn the persons of others, with which Jesus is gravely concerned.

On analysis our Lord's meaning might be stated as follows: If one arises at night and stubs his toe against the leg of the bed and kicks back at it, that is no sin. It may be considered by the psychologist a good example of infantilism or petulance! But it hurts no one save the toe of him who kicks. However, Jesus would say, one who stubs his toe against another's person and kicks at that person *even in thought or word* has committed sin, because that other person is in and of himself a sovereign entity made in the image of God. It is that image within him which makes him invulnerable against the attack of his fellows.

Just as the rabbis made up a series of penalties to match infringements against the law, it would seem, then, that our Lord here in ironical fashion sets a pattern for motivation infringements. In ironical fashion he suggests three gradations of penalty: (1) for anger, that one shall be liable to judgment of the court, although it is obvious that no court can deal with the motivation of the heart; (2) for addressing a brother as *reqa* or " empty head," that one shall be liable to be brought before the whole congregation of the people of God; (3) for crying out against a brother " *more* " or " heretic," that one shall be brought before the judgment bar of God whose condemnation is to be consigned to " fiery hell." [3]

It would seem obvious that this series of gradations of judgment is not to be taken seriously, as though a series of lower and higher courts could deal with one or another of the sins involved. For this reason we have spoken of the series as ironical on Jesus' part. What is even clearer is that here is a parallelism of structure in the stanza with its three parts suggestive of the fact that in the original Aramaic the statement was in poetical form. It seems also to be equally obvious that the entire stanza is concerned with the matter of inner attitudes and of the verbal expression of the same after a manner calculated to injure the sense of self-respect on the part of one so addressed. It is here that Jesus' concern lies.

The newly discovered Dead Sea scrolls contain several passages that are more suggestive of what Jesus has in mind at this point than anything in the writings of the rabbis, both with regard to the nature of sin and the penalty attaching thereto.

For example, much is made in these scrolls of the fact that the whole community, gathered together as an "assembly," is to judge all matters pertaining to the discipline of its members.[4] There is, for example, a striking similarity between the passage before us and the following from The Manual of Discipline:

> "One shall not speak to his brother in anger or in resentment, or with a stiff neck or a hard heart or a wicked spirit; one shall not hate him in the folly of his heart. In his days he shall reprove him and shall not bring upon him iniquity; and also a man shall not bring against his neighbor a word before the masters without having rebuked him before witnesses." [5]

One should perhaps gather from a comparison of our Lord's teachings at this point and that of the Qumran community that both are deeply concerned with the matter of attitude, because both in the latter and in the Christian church which our Lord was founding, it was essential that inner attitudes be right in order that such a well-knit community might survive.

> "If, then, you are presenting your offering at the altar
>> And there are reminded that your brother holds animosity against you,
>> Leave your offering there at the altar,
>> Go, first effect a reconciliation with your brother,
>> Then, come, present your offering."
>> (Matt. 5:23 f.)

Possibly one should see a connection between this paragraph of our Lord's teaching and the above quotation from The Manual of Discipline, in which we read of possible "resentment" and hatred in one's heart against his brother. Matthew Black has pointed out that in the Syriac versions at this point the reading is, "And there are reminded that your brother holds animosity (akh^{e}tha) against you." [6] If the Syriac represents the Aramaic correctly and the Qumran scroll and our Lord are both dealing with the matter of hatred or animosity in the heart of one's brother, then it is striking that they appear to solve the problem in much the same way! It is true that the Qumran scroll legislates that one shall " reprove " his brother for such an attitude, whereas Jesus suggests merely that "reconciliation with your brother" be made. But in both cases it is the inner attitude that is stressed rather than the importance of the overt act. How reconciliation is to be made our Lord does not state, but possibly we should imagine that the procedure is that outlined in Matt. 18:16 f., a procedure adopted from Deut. 19:15, and not unlike that suggested in the quotation from The Manual of Discipline.

It is striking that Jesus suggests the necessity of reconciliation with one's brother before one's worship is to be thought as acceptable to God. This seems very much like an endeavor to say that there cannot be a real conflict between one's religious duty, on the one hand, and one's ethical duty, on the other. If such a conflict appears to be involved in a given situation, Jesus suggests that the ethical duty be performed first and that thereafter the religious one be borne in mind. God, so to speak, does not want those to worship and serve him who are at odds with their brothers.

The far-reaching character of such teaching is sufficiently obvious. It amounts to saying that one may well show his love to God through his love to his fellow who is made in God's image. Saint Augustine is reported to have remarked that the whole of the Christian religion and ethics is to be summed up in this: " Love God and do as you please." Bearing in mind that when one loves one's brother one is actually loving the image of God in that brother, we may equally say that the whole of the Christian faith is made up of this: " Love your brother and do as you please! " In both cases, it is the quality and far-reaching character of love which serves to define one's attitude to God and man, so that one may in both cases add the imperative: " and do as you please! " One who properly loves God and his brother will only please that which, on the one hand, pleases God, and, on the other hand, blesses his fellow men.

" Come quickly to terms with your opponent,
While with him on the road,

Lest your opponent drag you before a judge,
　　The judge commit you to an officer of the court,
　　The officer throw you into jail.
Truly I tell you,
　　' You will never get out of there till you have paid out
　　your last cent! ' "

(Matt. 5:25 f.)

The concluding paragraph in our passage deals with a second situation which Matthew appears to have thought as relevant to the principle that Jesus discussed under the present heading regarding anger. T. W. Manson has shown that in the parallel passage at Luke 12:58 f. the situation supposed here has an eschatological setting that is more appropriate to its theme.[7] In the Lucan context the saying follows one in which Jesus speaks of men being able to discern the weather signs and then remarks, " You hypocrites, you know how to interpret the face of the earth and heaven; but how is it that you know not how to interpret this time? " As Manson remarks, " The moral of the parable is sufficiently obvious " in this eschatological context. For in these last times in which we live, men are now, so to speak, " on their way to the court," that is, to the judgment bar of God. If in a similar case they were on their way to be judged by man's court, they would leave no stone unturned to come to terms with an adversary with whom they realized they had no adequate case to present in court. Surely, no man has an adequate case with which he may come into the court of the Judge of all! Let a man, then, see the absolute necessity of coming to terms with his " opponent " before he arrives at the final bar of God.

If this interpretation is correct, as one is inclined to believe, the only problem that remains is as to the identity of the " opponent " in the case. This opponent, in the eschatological situation, will, so to speak, be the demand made by the presence of the Kingdom of God (which has come already in Jesus) upon the allegiance or loyalty of men. And Jesus' meaning in the saying will be that it is imperative that all who hear this demand made upon them respond in allegiance to the claims of God's Lordship over their lives. Let them quickly come to terms with this opponent lest they be dragged before the bar of God and committed by him to the punishment meted out to unruly spirits!

Chapter VI

Respecting the Other Sex

You have received by tradition the saying to men of old,
  " Thou shalt not commit adultery."
I say to you, however,
  " Everyone contemplating a woman with a lustful look
  Thereby commits adultery with her at heart."

If, then, your right eye cause your downfall,
    Gouge it out! Away with it!
    It is expedient for you that one of your members perish,
    Not that all your body be flung into hell!
If, again, your hand cause your downfall,
    Amputate it! Away with it!
    It is expedient for you that one of your members perish,
    Not that all your body be flung into hell!

Moreover, it has been said,
  " Whoever divorces his wife,
  Let him give her a bill of divorcement."
I say to you, however,
  " Everyone divorcing his wife (unless the ground be adultery),
  Makes her an adulteress.
  (Whoever marries a woman divorced commits adultery.) "
                                                    (Matt. 5:27–32.)

At the present juncture in his discourse, our Lord, with a view to indicating what it means to be merciful to another person, begins an analysis of the meaning of personality. His analysis lays hold first of the most fundamental distinction which men recognize in human personality, namely, that of sex. The

old law itself in the sequence of the Sixth and Seventh Commandments (Ex. 20:13–14) had followed the order "Thou
shalt not kill," "Thou shalt not commit adultery," and our
Lord finds it convenient to maintain this sequence. As before
also, he opens with the common rabbinic expression, "You have
heard that it was said," meaning, as we have already seen, "You
have received [by way of tradition] the saying that." [1]

But though our Lord follows the order of the Mosaic law in
his analysis of personality, his teaching on the subject, as we
shall see, is far more drastic than that ever accepted within the
sphere of Judaism. It is, in effect that sex is a factor of no importance in the matter of the reverence demanded by God for
human personality. He accepts the law's analysis of personality
into male and female only with a view to making this point
abundantly clear.

Adultery is the expression in its most extreme form of man's
desire to control the personality of another — the true sadism.
It is the expression, not of love for another's person, but rather
of lust to control that person for one's selfish ends. For in love
there is the acknowledgment of responsibility to match privilege
involved in association with another; in lust there is the desire
only for privilege with no thought of assuming the responsibility to match it.

All this one might well assume is at least implicit in the law's
teaching about the relations between the sexes.[2] But it is
doubtful whether contemporary Judaism, particularly that expressed by the dominant school of Pharisaism, ever went even
as far as this implicit teaching about the rights of women would
seem to demand, as we shall see when we come to the subject
of divorce. However this may be, at all events our Lord goes
beyond this point which is implicit in the Old Testament teaching. For as in his teaching with regard to murder and anger
in the preceding chapter, he now takes us again into the field
of intention or of motivation. As before, he is by no means satisfied merely to deal with the overt act as such but would proceed
to examine the attitude lying behind the sinful act.

" I say to you, however,
    ' Everyone contemplating a woman with a lustful look
    Thereby commits adultery with her at heart.' "

(Matt. 5:28.)

Such is our Lord's startling teaching! Karl Barth has some-where remarked that it is such teaching of Jesus which makes all men adulterers. This may appear too strong, but certainly it is no more than to say — as Jesus has already done — that all who are angry with or hate the persons of their fellow men are potential murderers at heart.

Perhaps Martin Luther's well-known saying represents more accurately our Lord's meaning: " I cannot keep the birds from alighting on my head, but I can restrain them from making nests in my hair." For our Lord is certainly not endeavoring to say that the sexual instinct, which is the common possession (and rightly) of both men and women, is in itself evil. On the contrary, he has much to say of the proper employment of the marriage relationship (Mark 10:4–12). It is not the sexual in-stinct with which his criticism deals but rather its lustful em-ployment, its leading one to the point of desiring to dominate over the person of another, enjoying privilege without offering matching responsibility.

It is this attitude which properly defines the word " lust," and it is this which our Lord roundly condemns. When such a sadistic attitude as this expresses itself in the overt act of adultery, man's laws take account of such sadism and it be-comes a crime punishable by the state. Neither here nor else-where, however, is our Lord interested in " crimes." His interest is always in " sin " and his point lies in this: that sin consists in inner attitude whereas crime consists in overt or outward act. Many a man would never think of committing an act of adultery because of the social mores of the group to which he belongs, whereas he would freely cultivate an inner lustful atti-tude which, if given an opportunity, would break out in the overt act.

" If, then, your right eye cause your downfall,
Gouge it out! Away with it!
It is expedient for you that one of your members perish,
Not that all your body be flung into hell!
If, again, your hand cause your downfall,
Amputate it! Away with it!
It is expedient for you that one of your members perish,
Not that all your body be flung into hell! "

(Matt. 5:29 f.)

It is possible, as T. W. Manson has suggested,[3] that in the original " M " Sermon, Jesus' teaching regarding the spirit or motivation with reference to the other sex concludes his teaching on adultery. This would seem to be the more likely perhaps, inasmuch as the two following short paragraphs under the present heading are found elsewhere, in substance at any rate, in Matthew's Gospel. Moreover, the teaching in these two short paragraphs is taken from Matthew's Marcan source, and Matthew's use of that source in the other passages concerned more closely follows the original (see Mark 9:43–47 and Matt. 18:8 f. for vs. 29 and 30; and for vs. 31 f., see Mark 10:4–12 and Matt. 19:3–9).

There are, however, significant differences between the text before us, on the one hand, and the use that Matthew makes of Mark in the other two passages, on the other. It is just possible, therefore, that Jesus himself reproduced the sayings in question for his purposes in the " M " Sermon. Moreover, it is to be observed, as Vincent Taylor remarks, that the first of the two short paragraphs as found in Mark 9:43–47 represents a portion of a group of sayings whose order does not go back to Jesus himself, but rather appears to have been " compiled under a catechetical impulse by the aid of catchwords intended to assist the memory." [4] Reference to Mark 9:37–50 exhibits a group of sayings of our Lord in poetical parallelism whose only connection with one another is due to the presence " of the catchwords ' cause to stumble,' ' good,' and ' cast,' " together with others like " in my name," " be flung into hell," and " to enter into life," which serve to bind portions of the group of sayings together. In view of these considerations it would seem permissible to assume that the teachings in the two short paragraphs before us in our Lord's mind have a bearing upon the problem of adultery.

Assuming this to be the case, we notice that Matthew quotes in this passage but two of the three sayings in Mark concerned with the part that members of the body may play in one's moral and spiritual downfall. In the Marcan passage the members concerned are the " hand," " foot," and " eye," in this order. In the present context, however, only the " eye " and " hand " are referred to, no doubt because only they are concerned in the sin of adultery with which our Lord here is dealing. The eye invokes the temptation and the hand performs the act of sin as the result of acquiescence.

Some account must be taken of the exceedingly drastic exhortation that Jesus gives his disciples in such cases: " Gouge it out! Away with it! " " Amputate it! Away with it! " One hears occasionally of instances of his followers who have taken his teaching quite literally at this point and have performed the sort of amputation indicated! To do so, however, is at once to overlook the fact of the generally parabolic nature of our Lord's teaching, on the one hand, and of the Jewish ethos in which it is given, on the other.

The Hebrew psychology took its start from the account in Gen., ch. 2, of God's creation of man, which taught that his life was a unified existence made up of a body of " dust " into which God had blown the " breath of life." Unlike the Greek thought of our Lord's day which held to a dichotomy in man's being — that is, that he was made up of two separable elements, body and soul — contemporary Judaism taught that the breath or spirit blown by God into man had permeated every portion of his body. In consequence, there was no portion of that body not filled with spirit.[5]

Long before the discovery of the circulation of the blood, therefore, Judaism taught that a blemish in any part of man's personality might easily be communicated to every other part and thus vitiate the whole. It is against such a background that our Lord says, " If, then, your right eye cause your downfall," and " if, again, your hand cause your downfall," gouge out the one, amputate the other! This, then, is a neat way of saying that sin in any quarter of one's person needs to be dealt with speedily and drastically lest the whole personality be vitiated and ultimately destroyed. And we are carried back in our thinking unmistakably to that inner sanctum of the personality with which Jesus here is particularly dealing, namely, " the heart " out of which are the issues of life. He could not well have said, " If your heart cause your downfall, gouge it out, away with it! " Hence, the use of eye and hand to serve his purpose.

Moreover, our Lord up to a point agrees in this passage with the current Jewish doctrine regarding the nature of the future life. That doctrine appears to have been that one would be raised up with the bodily defects that were his at death. That is to say, in the resurrection he would be found blind, lame, or otherwise maimed or deformed if he had been such in this life.[6] However, we should scarcely feel free to press his teaching literally at this point, any more than that at which we have just been looking regarding the amputation of one's members. In the current language of the day he is presenting what would be a splendid *argumentum ad hominem* for those Jews entertaining the sort of belief to which reference has just been made. In line with his teaching as a whole, we are to understand that he means that every sort of temptation is to be resisted that the personality as a whole may not be destroyed.

Incidentally, it is to be remarked that the word for " hell " used here by our Lord (*Gehenna*), save for James 3:6, is found in the New Testament only in his teachings.[7] *Gehenna* is actually a transliteration of the two Hebrew words *ge* and *hinnom*, meaning the valley of Hinnom to the west of Jerusalem in which garbage had been burned from the day of Josiah (II Kings 23:10). This name had long since come to stand for the portion of the abode of the dead allotted to the souls of the damned.[8] It would seem obvious, then, that this also is figurative language on Jesus' lips and is intended to indicate the danger of the destruction of personality by sin. The ultimate nature of that destruction is not divulged here or elsewhere in his teaching.

> " Moreover, it has been said,
>> ' Whoever divorces his wife,
>> Let him give her a bill of divorcement.'
> I say to you, however,
>> ' Everyone divorcing his wife (unless the ground be adultery),
>> Makes her an adulteress.
>> (Whoever marries a woman divorced commits adultery.) ' "
>
> (Matt. 5:31 f.)

In the third short paragraph of this section Jesus returns to the phraseology with which the section opens. The theme formed by the lines " it has been said " and " I say to you " is repeated. There is also a certain parallelism of structure in the couplets that follow in each case the " it has been said " and the " I say to you." Taken with the other two paragraphs of the section, therefore, it will be seen that this one nicely rounds it off in an unmistakable way and suggests that Jesus spent some time upon the composition of the section as a whole.

In the present paragraph it appears that Jesus is not endeavoring to deal with the whole problem of divorce as such. This he does in the passage at Mark 10:2–12 and its parallel in Matt. 19:3–12.[9] Here, on the contrary, his purpose is merely to suggest the effect of divorce in the destruction of the personality of the divorcee. This problem of the destruction of the divorcee's personality is not under consideration in the passage in Deut. 24:1 which was traditionally quoted as the ground for divorce in contemporary Jewish circles. It is this passage that Jesus is quoting in its traditional form when he remarks, " It has been said, ' Whoever divorces his wife, let him give her a bill of divorcement.' " The only concern at that passage was one of the proper etiquette involved in granting a divorce to his wife on a Jewish man's part! Previous to the law involved in the Deuteronomy passage, it had apparently been permissible for a man to dismiss his wife with some such statement as, "You are now divorced from me." Islamic law in fact even today permits the husband to divorce his wife with the thrice-repeated verbal formula: "You are divorced. You are divorced. You are divorced." Neither the Islamic nor the pre-Deuteronomic law required that a man go to law and secure a divorce against his wife in court.

Nor did the law at Deut. 24:1 make this requirement of the man. It did, however, cause him to stop and ponder on the result of his rash action to the extent of writing out a bill of divorcement and giving it to his wife. Nor did the Pharisaism contemporary with Jesus provide any more searching analysis of the effect of divorce on human personality than that provided in the law. Starting with Deut. 24:1, the interest of the Pharisees centered about a proper appraisal of what might be considered just grounds for divorce, as the following paragraph from the Mishnah will serve to indicate:

> "The School of Shammai say: A man may not divorce his wife unless he has found unchastity in her, for it is written, *Because he hath found in her* indecency *in anything*. And the School of Hillel say: (He may divorce her) even if she spoil a dish for him, for it is written, *because he hath found in her indecency* in anything."
>
> (M. Gittin 9:10)

But as was just said, Jesus' interest here is not in the grounds for divorce but in the effect of it upon the divorcee. This is as it should be, of course, in the context of the Sermon on the Mount in which Jesus is concerned with personality at every point. It seems rather futile, therefore, to compare the present passage with that of Mark 10:2-12 and Matt. 19:3-12, with a view to noting minutely any differences between them. For the topic under consideration in the latter passages is the permissibility of divorce as such — a problem of wider scope than that under consideration here.

Jesus' point in the present passage may be allowed to stand out in a rather startling way by slightly rearranging the quotation with which he is dealing and his reply to it, as follows:

The quotation — " Whoever divorces his wife,
                      Let him give her a bill of divorcement."
Jesus' reply   — " Everyone divorcing his wife,
                      Makes her an adulteress."

The startling contrast between the traditional teaching based on the law and our Lord's teaching relative to divorce's effect upon character is evident. His point is that when divorce dissolves marriage, it negates marriage. And a woman thus cast out upon the world without the protection that marriage provides makes of her a castoff, a chattel, one who has been made the object of man's lustful desire. We have already seen that it is this sort of sadism which is the adultery of the heart and against which Jesus delivers his strong invective. It is but one step farther — and he now takes it — to suggest that the stigma of such adultery attaches to that person upon whom wanton sadism has been practiced, rather than upon the culprit himself.

The law itself attempted to safeguard the woman from this evil result within Hebrew-Jewish society. Reference may be made, for example, to Deut. 25:8–10 and Ruth 4:7 ff. Jesus is not concerned with creating safeguards, however. His concern is with checking evil at the source by creating a right attitude between husband and wife and maintaining it.

In the present context the words in parentheses, " unless the ground be adultery," which are well supported by the manuscripts, should certainly be taken to mean that one who is already an adulteress is not made such by divorce. This is merely to say what our homely proverb suggests: that " one cannot spoil a bad egg." The last line of the teaching — " Whoever marries a woman divorced commits adultery " — breaks up the rhythm of the paragraph and probably has no place in Jesus' teaching at this point. It is omitted by the best manuscripts in the West.[10]

Chapter VII

The Mind and the Standard of Truth

Again, you have received by tradition the saying to men of old,
  "Thou shalt not break thy word given under oath:
  Rather, promises made under oath thou shalt fulfill for the
    Lord."

I say to you, however,
  "Wholly refrain from taking oath —
      Whether by heaven — for it is 'God's Throne,'
      Or by earth — for it is 'footstool for his feet,'
      Or by Jerusalem — for it is 'Capital of the Great King.'
  Nor take an oath by your head —
      For you have no power
      To make a single hair white or black.
  Rather, let your word 'yes' mean 'yes,' 'no' mean 'no' —
  Whatever exceeds these is of the Evil One."

(Matt. 5:33–37.)

In this and in the two succeeding chapters we are presented with our Lord's analysis of the inner life of man along lines that are familiar to the student of human psychology. The primitive psychology of the Semitic peoples, accepted by the Hebrew prophets and found throughout the Scriptures generally, held the heart of man to be the center of his being, from which " the issues of life " proceeded. The heart was generally taken to be the locus of what we ordinarily think of as mind, feelings, and will. The abdominal viscera (the liver, spleen, pancreas, and bowels) were also credited with a share of man's higher existence. In Scripture all of these are at times summed up under the Hebrew and Greek words for " viscera," the whole together being declared to be the source of such life.[1]

Our Lord in general accepted this popular psychology of the contemporary Judaism, as for example v. 28 above indicates. Instances are to be found in each of our Gospels and their sources in support of the thesis that he employed the word " heart " in contexts in which we should speak of the mind, the will, or the emotions or feelings. Examples taken almost at random from the Gospels exhibit his use of the word " heart " where we should use " will " (Mark 8:17; Matt. 11:29; Luke 16:15), " mind " (Mark 2:8; 7:21; 11:23; Matt. 24:48; Luke 6:45; John 13:2), or " the emotions " (Mark 12:30, 33; Matt. 5:28; 6:21; Luke 21:14, 34; John 14:1, 27; 16:6, 22). This is a mere selection from among many examples in our Lord's teaching, and the fact that they occur among all the witnesses may be taken as confirmation of his acceptance of the Hebrew psychology for all practical purposes.

This is not to say, however, that he did not distinguish in his thinking between the respective functions of what we term the mind, the feelings, and the will. On the contrary, that both he and his contemporaries recognized the functional distinctions within the inner life of man which we designate by these terms is clear from the pages of Scripture. And there is no clearer evidence of this than the passage Matt. 5:33–48, in which a threefold paragraphing is clearly indicated by the repetition of the clause to which we have now become accustomed: " You have received by tradition the saying to men of old " (see vs. 33, 38, and 43).

> " Again, you have received by tradition the saying to men of
>> old,
>> ' Thou shalt not break thy word given under oath:
>> Rather, promises made under oath thou shalt fulfill for
>> the Lord.' "
>
> (Matt. 5:33.)

The first of the three divisions of man's personality, then, to which our Lord calls our attention is that of the mind. The taking of an oath and the consequent binding of one's self to perform an act was considered a sacred thing among Semitic peoples from time immemorial. It was a common practice long before the exile to use the sacred name with a view to indicating the sanctity of the oath. The law contains numerous references to this practice and to the fact that God will hold a man guilty who breaks his oath taken in this way. The following quotations will serve to illustrate this fact:

> " You shall not take the name of the Lord your God in vain; for the Lord will not hold him guiltless who takes his name in vain."
>
> (Ex. 20:7.)

> " And you shall not swear by my name falsely, and so profane the name of your God: I am the Lord."
>
> (Lev. 19:12.)

To take oath in this way, and particularly to use one of the sacred names in doing so, was considered so seriously that the practice arose for one to adjure another to take oath with regard to anything under discussion between two persons. A good example of this practice is found in I Kings 2:36–46. Solomon, it would appear, had adjured Shimei by an oath that he should dwell in Jerusalem and not depart from the city without his knowledge at any time. Three years later, however, when two of Shimei's slaves ran away, the latter rode his ass down to Gath and then to Achish in search of the slaves. When Solomon heard of this, he summoned Shimei and demanded of him, " Did I not make you swear by the Lord, and solemnly admonish you, saying, ' Know for certain that on the day you go forth and go to any place whatever, you shall die '? "

An oath taken in this way was termed " the oath of the Lord " (II Sam. 21:7). Its purpose will appear to have been twofold: first, to insure a sense of the solemnness of the oath through the use of the divine name, and secondly, by bringing the name of the Lord into the transaction to make doubly sure the fulfillment of the act to which the oath referred, as it was now something pledged " as unto the Lord."

It is true that there is no specific statement made in the law to the effect that " promises made under oath thou shalt fulfill for the Lord." Psalm 50:14, which is often cited in this connection, refers not to *oaths* but rather to *vows* — that is, to religious obligations undertaken with a view to dedicating one's self in a specific way to the service of God, on the one hand, or to abstaining from certain things or acts that were ordinarily considered permissible, on the other.[2] However, it would seem that passages like Ex. 20:7 and Lev. 19:12 above quoted would speak strongly for themselves to the Jewish mind. It is likely, therefore, that in the present passage our Lord unconsciously uses the language of Ps. 50:14 pertaining to *vows* and applies it to *oaths* in a manner that would have been acceptable in his day.[3]

> " I say to you, however,
>   ' Wholly refrain from taking oath —
>   Whether by heaven — for it is " God's Throne,"
>   Or by earth — for it is " footstool for his feet,"
>   Or by Jerusalem — for it is " Capital of the Great
>   King."
>   Nor take an oath by your head —
>   For you have no power
>   To make a single hair white or black.
>   Rather, let your word " yes " mean " yes," " no " mean
>   " no " —
>   Whatever exceeds these is of the Evil One.' "
>   (Matt. 5:34–37.)

The whole subject of oaths and vows is extensively treated in the rabbinical literature of from two to four centuries following our Lord's day. That treatment undoubtedly in large part follows the teachings on these subjects of the scribes contemporary with Jesus himself. In Mishnah and Talmud, the two books Shebuoth (oaths) and Nedarim (vows) deal extensively with these two subjects. In view of our Lord's suggestion that his disciples should refrain from taking oath " by heaven," " by earth," " by Jerusalem," " by your head," and the like, it is instructive to read a paragraph like the following in the Mishnah:

" (If a man said,) ' I adjure you ' or ' I command you,' or ' I bind you,' they are liable. (But if he said,) ' By heaven and by earth,' they are exempt. (If he adjured them) ' by Alef-Daleth ' or ' by Yod-He ' or ' by Shaddai ' or ' by Sabaoth ' or ' by the Merciful and Gracious' or ' by him that is long-suffering and of great kindness,' or by any substituted name, they are liable. If a man cursed (God) by any of these, he is liable. So R. Meir. But the Sages say: He is exempt. If a man cursed his father or his mother by any of these names, he is liable. So R. Meir. But the Sages declare him exempt."

(M. Shebuoth 4:13.)

It is also generally apropos to note that in the making of vows, the lamb of the daily whole offering in the temple, the wood for burning on the altar, the fire offerings themselves, the altar, Jerusalem, and the like, were brought into play and vows were made in the name of each of these.[4]

This practice of taking oath by the use of the divine names or some substitute for them, which was common in Jesus' day, is characteristic of the Semitic culture generally. It is a common practice at the present day all over the Arabic world with its Semitic cultural background. Not alone the divine names, but any object considered sacred by the one who swears or the one who demands the swearing by an oath, is employed in this connection. The motivation behind this practice is quite different from that connected with the so-called " cursing words " employed by Westerners. No doubt in the use of such words there is a relic of a like practice even in the West. But if such is the case, the underlying motivation has by and large been forgotten in the Western hemisphere. The nearest approach to the motivation intended in the Semitic world is found in the taking of an oath in our Western courts, where one who swears is asked to raise his hand or to place it upon the Bible. The intention in all these and like cases is, of course, to assure that he who swears upon that which he holds most sacred will be constrained to tell " the truth, the whole truth, and nothing but the truth."

A similar motivation lies behind the Semitic practice of taking oath with reference to anyone or anything that the oath-taker considers sacred. It is intended thereby that a liar shall thus be turned *ipso facto* into a truthteller! Jesus knew, however, as many who have lived for any length of time in the Semitic culture have long since discovered, that no liar is thus converted into a teller of the truth. There is one way, and one way only, that this feat may be accomplished. This is by instilling into the heart of man a reverence for the truth for its own sake. And there can be no doubt that this is the meaning of Jesus' injunction in the passage " Rather, let your word ' yes ' mean ' yes,' ' no ' mean ' no ' — whatever exceeds these is of the Evil One."

It is so that James, who seems to have had before him in the form of oral tradition much of Jesus' teaching, understood this saying. For he seems to be referring to it when he says, " Moreover, above all, my brothers, do not swear at all, neither by heaven nor by earth nor by any other oath; but let your ' no ' be ' no ' and your ' yes ' be ' yes,' lest you fall under judgment " (James 5:12).

Jesus' meaning, then, will be that which is enshrined in our homely proverb: " Let your word be as good as your bond." And once again we observe, as throughout the Sermon, that our Lord is interested in attitudes, in inner motivation, in the condition of the heart, rather than in the outer word or act. His earnest wish is that the mind of his follower shall earnestly pursue the cause of truth because this alone is right.[5]

Incidentally, the expression in Greek which is translated " of the Evil One " may equally well be translated " of evil." Whether our Lord here and elsewhere, after the fashion of his day in Jewish circles and that of the later Christian church, is personifying evil is a question open to dispute. (See the discussion on the subject below at Matt. 6:13.)

CHAPTER VIII

The Will and Dedicated Humility

You have received by tradition the saying,
   " Eye for eye, tooth for tooth."

I say to you, however,
   " Offer no resistance to an evil person.
      Rather —
         Whoever slaps you on your cheek (the right one),
         Turn to him also the other!
         Whoever would drag you into court to take your shirt,
         Let him have your coat as well!
         Whoever would force you to serve him for a mile,
         Go with him yet two others!
         Whoever would beg of you,
         Make him a donation!
         Whoever would borrow of you,
         Turn not from him! "

(Matt. 5:38–42.)

After dealing with the problem of the mind and the standard of truth that it obeys, our Lord now turns to the second major portion of man's personality which the Hebrew included in the term " heart," namely, the will. And as with the mind, so here the problem is at once how to maintain one's own self-respect and at the same time respect one's fellow, how to dedicate one's will to the service of God and one's fellow men.

Moreover, like the scribes of his day, our Lord begins with the traditional use made of the Mosaic law in the contemporary Jewish culture. The saying that he quotes is found in more than one passage in the Pentateuch. Its clearest statement perhaps, and certainly that which best indicates its relevance in the contemporary culture of the time in which it was uttered, is to be found at Lev. 24:19 f.: " When a man causes a disfigurement in his neighbor, as he has done it shall be done to him, fracture for fracture, eye for eye, tooth for tooth; as he has disfigured a man, he shall be disfigured." [1]

It seems clear that the original intent of the law in the Mosaic legislation was to secure something like equity in a man's dealings with his fellow men. Without such legislation, man's emotions are generally given full sway and, as we say, " take over." If, in the course of a private clash between individuals, one man knocked out his neighbor's eye, that neighbor felt free under the stress of the occasion to strike off the other's head! So also if his tooth was knocked out or if he was in any way disfigured. In such circumstances the purpose of the Mosaic legislation was clearly to establish a sense of equity in such matters; so that the penalty might be made to fit the crime. This was only reasonable and right, when one considers that the Mosaic legislation was made, as all laws are made in any culture, with a view to doing away with the anarchy of the cave man! The natural man in any cultural environment reverts to the cave man when left entirely to himself. It is the avowed purpose of law to act as a deterrent against this normal reversal in all societies.

The Mishnah, which as the lawbook developed by the rabbis of the early Christian centuries contains the " traditions of the elders " of Jesus' own day and previously, has for its major motivation the application of the Mosaic legislation to the contemporary scene. Its relation to that legislation may be expressed by the algebraic ratio: as is constitutional law to statutory law, so is the Mosaic legislation to that of Mishnah and Talmud. In other words, Mishnah and Talmud endeavor to apply the Mosaic legislation in life situations. In dealing with Deut. 19:21, therefore — a passage parallel to the one we have just cited from Leviticus — the Mishnah makes the following application:

" Scripture says, ' *Life for life*; thus they are not put to death until judgment [of death] has been given [against him that was falsely accused] ' " (M. Makkoth 1:6).

From this and like passages that might be quoted from the Mishnah and Talmud almost ad infinitum, it becomes clear that the height of the Pharisaic rabbis' ambition was to apply the Mosaic legislation in the culture of his day. When one grants the premise that the Mosaic legislation was given to the Hebrew-Jewish people to serve the purpose of securing equity and justice in their social life through the centuries, as the Pharisees held, the application of that legislation by Mishnah and Talmud is readily seen to have been a laudable ambition. The like promulgation of statutory laws on the part of our legislators in this country, in the light of and in accordance with the general principles laid down by our Constitution and Declaration of Independence, is obviously a necessary function in our organized society.

Equity of the " eye for eye, tooth for tooth, life for life " type is generally called in legal terminology the *jus talionis*. Strack-Billerbeck hold that the evidence is not clear that in Jesus' day the rabbis actually insisted on the literal carrying out of the Mosaic legislation at this point. These writers suggest that the evidence indicates that only Rabbi Eliezer, who flourished about A.D. 90, held to a literal understanding of the phrase " an eye for an eye." [2] Certainly, however, if the rabbis did not take the law with such literal seriousness, with their background and motivation they had every right to do so! This problem, however, is of no great concern to us here as Jesus neither here nor elsewhere suggests that the scribes of his day pushed such a law of equity to its ultimate possible conclusion.

> " I say to you, however,
>   ' Offer no resistance to an evil person.' "
>   (Matt. 5:39.)

But however legitimate may be the setting up of statutory legislation on the basis of predetermined constitutional law, our Lord's motivation in his ethical teaching was quite other-wise. He was concerned with a deterrent to sin which goes far deeper than any legislation can hope to do and affects the very source springs of man's ethical life. His aim was not to do away with the claims of equity and justice in a duly-constituted soci-ety. Rather, it was to touch the vital center from which man's attitudes toward his fellow spring. This is the human will.

" I say to you, however," he says, " ' Offer no resistance to an evil person.' " Here is a maxim intended to strike a far more telling blow for the problem of human relations than any mere legislation is capable of doing. Equity may be right and proper in its way in an organized society. But no law of equity can possibly bring about right relations between men. On the con-trary, the application of such a law may have exactly the oppo-site effect in practice. The " blood feud," found in many cul-tures, has been the result of the endeavor to secure equity as between man and man, family and family, clan and clan. Even in cultural situations or societies in which adequate legislation has been found, the principle of " a life for a life " has led to the feud being handed down from father to son for generations. Human nature being what it is, therefore, what appears right in theory does not always result in attaining the ends of justice in practice.

No society has successfully solved the problem of eliminating that type of individual from its midst who remains unsatisfied, though the law of equity be functioning smoothly and with pre-cision. It is not equity that the criminally minded want. Nor is it equity that those who desire to save face seek. There are springs of evil in man's nature from which flow those forces which would gladly destroy both equity and justice. It is those springs with which Jesus would deal because if the bitter waters of jealousy and envy, of vengeance and hatred, which are found to flow from them may be stopped at the source, then not only will the ends of equity and justice be served, but the more com-prehensive issues of man's total relation with his fellow man will also be resolved.

It is with these deeper springs of character that our Lord is dealing when he says, " Offer no resistance to an evil person." This is to suggest that one's will is not to be pitted against another's will, that one is rather to think more highly of one's neighbor than one thinks of self, that one is to place the possession of eye or tooth on the neighbor's part above one's own possession of eye or tooth. One is to realize that in an imperfect world in which sin is rampant in all of man's relations with his fellow man, a certain give-and-take is required whose claims exceed those of the law of equity. One is to accept the fact that, though it is true that " all men are created equal," in a sinful world one cannot make a practice of going about and demanding the rights which such equality entails. Indeed, in man's social relations with his fellow man, the problem of securing one's rights must not be constantly to the fore at all.

It is not too much to say that in our Lord's teaching of such an absolute ethic the word " rights " has no place. To go about at all times demanding that one's " rights " be observed by one's fellows may accord with the law of equity. Such practice does not accord with the motivation at the heart of the Christian ethic. The Christian ethic demands rather that one place the rights of one's fellow above one's own.[3]

No doubt to demand vengeance upon someone's misconduct against oneself is to accord with the law of simple equity. And no doubt before the law one has every right to do so. Even to observe the policy that one will await revenge because God has said, " Vengeance is mine, and recompense" (Deut. 32:35) is no doubt in accordance with a strictly legalistic attitude. But all this is definitely sub-Christian. It is even arguable that such a spirit is below the standard of the Mosaic legislation itself (Lev. 19:18). But the Christian ethic at all events demands that one shall not even desire the Lord's vengeance to be exercised against one's neighbor or one's enemy. One, therefore, does not pray that the Lord will wreak vengeance on one's enemy, but rather repeats the prayer of our Lord himself: " Father, forgive them; for they know not what they do " (Luke 23:34).

An ethic placing one's rights or one's equity on a par with the rights and equity of one's fellows is obviously a crossless ethic. It is an ethic that refuses to accept slander against one's fair name, a blow at one's pride, an infringement of one's rights. Such an ethic Jesus neither taught nor lived. Rather, he both taught and lived an ethic that placed a cross in the center of one's every experience with one's fellows. Accordingly, his own relations with his fellow men placed him upon a cross. And he equally taught his disciples of every age: "Whoever does not bear his own cross and come after me, cannot be my disciple" (Luke 14:27).

It is, then, in accordance with our Lord's entire teaching and practice to observe that in the present passage he means for his disciple to bend his will to the will of his fellow. Such an ethic as our Lord's is one that may properly be termed "the art of ethical sublimation." It is an ethic that submerges the rights of the individual human will in a far perspective taking account above all else of the overarching will of God.

> "Rather —
>> Whoever slaps you on your cheek (the right one),
>> Turn to him also the other!
>> Whoever would drag you into court to take your shirt,
>> Let him have your coat as well!
>> Whoever would force you to serve him for a mile,
>> Go with him yet two others!
>> Whoever would beg of you,
>> Make him a donation!
>> Whoever would borrow of you,
>> Turn not from him! "

(Matt. 5:39–42.)

At this point Matthew introduces five illustrations of the principle with which we have been dealing. Luke also gives us four of the five illustrations but places them after the injunction to love one's enemies which occurs in Matthew in the next section, with which we are to deal in Chapter IX (see Luke 6:27–31 and Matt. 5:43–48). Similarly Luke attaches the so-called "Golden Rule" to this series of illustrations in ch.

6:31, whereas Matthew places it at ch. 7:12. In addition to the problem of placement of Matthew's five illustrations, there is another relating to the nature of their exact wording. Luke's choice of words suggests on the whole a series of illustrations relating to physical violence, whereas Matthew's leaves the impression that our Lord was concerned here rather with matters of insult and litigation, and the like.

The first of these problems need not long detain us. The present writer is inclined to believe that the Lucan placement is more likely to be correct. In the Sermon on the Mount, Jesus is inculcating a right attitude toward one's neighbor, as we have had occasion in several places to observe, and it would seem, therefore, that these examples would fit in most readily after the injunction to love one's enemies. However, the placing of the five illustrations at the point chosen by Matthew is only less natural than that in Luke. For while our Lord deals, it is true, with the personality under its three aspects of mind, will, and emotions, it would be a mistake to suppose that he wishes to trichotomize human personality into hard and fast compartments. As we shall see in the chapter that immediately follows, " love " is for him a matter of the *will* and not only of the *emotions*; so, to suggest that the will could properly be motivated without the presence of an attitude of love in the heart of his disciple would be entirely to misunderstand Jesus' teaching.

The second problem pertaining to the probable originality of one or other form of the sayings (that of Matthew or that of Luke) is not so easily resolved. The problem here concerns to some extent the probable originality of the one or the other form in the Aramaic which our Lord was speaking. And here, unfortunately, the pandits appear to differ. C. F. Burney, followed by T. W. Manson, finds the Lucan version to be cast the more readily into Aramaic poetical form, exhibiting parallelism, rhyme, and rhythm.[4] On the other hand, Matthew Black suggests that " Luke's editorial work consists of an accommodation of his Jewish material to Gentile ways of thought," and he concludes that the Lucan form here is not necessarily " the more faithful to the Aramaic original." [5]

The present writer finds Matthew Black's arguments rather convincing. This, then, argues for the general originality of Matthew's wording in the form before us. In the nature of the case, such results as are derived from a probable Aramaic original, however, in the present state of our knowledge can be held only as tentative. In any case, there is no conclusive argument available for our Lord's not having presented these illustrations at one time or another in both the Matthean and Lucan forms. We therefore proceed to a short examination of them as they lie before us.

In these five examples Jesus applies as follows the principle with which he has been dealing regarding the will:

1. *The insulting slap:* as has been frequently pointed out, a slap to the right cheek must perforce have been given by the back of the right hand. This, as T. W. Manson has pointed out, was considered by the rabbis as peculiarly insulting. M. Baba Kamma 8:6 reads: " If he slapped him, he must pay him 200 zuz. If [he struck him] with *the back of his hand,* he must pay him 400 zuz." (Italics mine.) The same paragraph in the Mishnah suggests that this backhand slap is as serious as tearing off a man's ear, plucking out his hair, or spitting on him, and goes on to remark that the general rule is: " All is in accordance with a person's honor." In accordance with the principle of Christian conduct, however, which we have been noting in this section, our Lord enjoins that his disciple is to present to an enemy the left cheek for a like insulting slap!

2. *The case of litigation:* here, as before, the Christian is not to seek equity but rather to reply to litigation with aggressive love. One cannot doubt that Paul in his practical dealing with the church in a later period has caught the spirit of his master, when he teaches his converts: " To have lawsuits at all with one another is defeat for you. Why not rather suffer wrong? Why not rather be defrauded? " (I Cor. 6:7.)

3. *Impressment for service:* the Greek word employed here is one that refers to drafting for military service on the part of an

invading army. And Jesus suggests that, to use this military term
in the widest possible context, all impressment is to be answered
by the law of love, the Christian disciple going far beyond the
demands made upon him. There is good evidence for suggesting that our Lord here said for his disciples to go two miles beyond the requirement made upon them. The case becomes that
of three to one then, rather than of two to one as suggested in
the usual translation.[6]

4. *The matter of begging:* begging in the Semitic world is *a
fine art!* So much is this the case that one may almost say that
this fourth illustration is the hardest for someone who knows
the East to take quite literally! The cry of " *bakhsheesh* " has
for centuries been the most irritating to travelers in the Middle
East. Moreover, one realizes from long living in the Orient that
to give in response to this cry is to underwrite an institution
that is degrading to human personality. But our Lord's illustration here is not to be taken literally any more than is any of
the others. He is far from desiring to perpetuate an institution
that would destroy the very end that he is seeking to promote.
His point as always is to submit one's will to the will of another in so far as that submission will serve to enrich and bring
to maturity the person of the other.

5. *The matter of loans:* the necessity for borrowing is limited to no culture nor to any single financial situation. But
wherever lending is put on a financial basis, the result is either
repayment with interest or even usury. Probably our Lord's
meaning, therefore, in this passage is best served by reference to
the parallel at Luke 6:34: " And if you lend to them of whom
you hope to receive, what thank have you? For sinners also
lend to sinners, to receive as much again." Jesus is suggesting,
then, that when one makes a loan, one is not to raise the problem of its return either with interest or usury. Sinners make
loans of this type! Jesus' disciples are to go beyond the customs
of sinners and to submit their wills once again in love to the will
of the other man.

Nothing could be more heart-searching than the teaching

contained in the passage before us in this chapter. If, as our modern psychologists tell us, the will is the focal point of the personality, is indeed the person himself, then Jesus has here sought out the springs of ethical conduct. And his point will be throughout that his disciple is so to motivate his will at all times with reference to his fellow man that the good of that other may be his constant concern.

CHAPTER IX

The Emotions and God's Universalism

You have received by tradition the saying,
  " Thou shalt love thy neighbor;
  Thou shalt hate thine enemy."

I say to you, however,
    " Love your enemies!
    Pray for your persecutors
        That you may become sons of your Father in heaven,
        Who makes his sun rise on evil and good,
        Who causes his rain to fall on righteous and unrighteous.
    For if you conceive love for those who love you,
        What thanks can you expect?
        Do not even collaborationists as much?
    And if you are on speaking terms with your ' brothers ' only,
        Wherein are you surpassing the rest of men?
        Do not even they as much?

Be adults, then,
As your Heavenly Father is of perfect stature."

(Matt. 5:43–48.)

Jesus now turns to the third element in man's personality — his emotional life. Of the traditional saying which Jesus takes as his starting point in the discussion, the first part — " Thou shalt love thy neighbor " — is taken literally from Lev. 19:18. The second part of the saying — " Thou shalt hate thine enemy " — however, is to be found nowhere in the scriptures of the Old Testament. The suggestion has been made that the two clauses

99

as taken together represent, no doubt, a " popular maxim " current in Jesus' day.[1]

It is scarcely necessary, however, to substantiate Jesus' use of the saying in this double form by reference to a hypothetical popular maxim. To hate one's enemy is the normative response of any man sharing the corporate sin of the race! Moreover, it is a truism that " actions speak louder than words," and the recorded dealings of ancient Israel and Judah with their enemies were very much of a piece with those of the other nations contemporary with them.[2] Moreover, it is rather generally agreed, one imagines, that though the passage Lev. 19:18 has been designated " the highest point in the ethics of the Old Testament," [3] yet " by the neighbor " is meant a fellow Israelite.[4] The parallelism in the verse which serves to define its two parts is itself suggestive of such a conclusion: " You shall not take vengeance or bear any grudge against the sons of your own people, but you shall love your neighbor as yourself: I am the Lord " (Lev. 19:18). This must be remembered when it is said, for example, that Rabbi Akiba found in Lev. 19:18 " the most comprehensive rule in the law," [5] or that " Rabbi Jose, a disciple of Rabban Johanan ben Zakkai (A.D. 80), endeavored to implement the Levitical rule by saying, ' Let thy neighbor's property be as dear to thee as thine own,' " [6] and that Rabbi Eliezer did the same with his application — " Let the honor of thy fellow be as dear to thee as thine own." [7]

There is abundant proof of this so-called " particularism " on the part of the Pharisees and their rabbis contemporary with Jesus.[8] Sufficient evidence of this fact is to be found in a single quotation from M. Sanhedrin 10:1. The passage reads in part: " All Israelites have a share in the world to come. . . . And these are they that have no share in the world to come: he that says there is no resurrection of the dead prescribed in the law, and (he that says) that the law is not from heaven and an Epicurean." Regarding this last category Canon Danby aptly remarks that this is — " a frequent epithet applied both to Gentiles and Jews opposed to rabbinical teachings." [9]

It is undoubtedly this situation with which our Lord was dealing in his so-called parable of the good Samaritan at Luke
10:29–37. In the context of the Pharisaic particularism as over
against Jesus' universalism, the question addressed to him by
the Pharisaic lawyer — " And who is my neighbor? " — was entirely apropos. And it is clear from Jesus' reply that for him
the " neighbor " is every man, regardless of race or class or
creed. A new day had dawned within the contemporary Jewish
culture when Jesus made such a pronouncement.[10]

> " I say to you, however,
>   ' Love your enemies! ' "
>
> (Matt. 5:44.)

As we turn now to Jesus' positive teaching on the subject, it
will be well for us to have before us not only the traditional
form of Jesus' teaching as presented by Matthew but also that
to be found in Luke 6:27–33. The passage in Luke may be translated as follows:

> " I say to you that are listening,
>   ' Love your enemies!
>   Treat well those who hate you!
>   Bless those who curse you!
>   Pray for those who offer violence to you! . . .
>   If you conceive love for those who love you,
>   What thanks is this to you?
>   For even sinners love those who love them!
>   If you treat well those who treat you well,
>   What thanks is this to you?
>   For even sinners do the same.' " [11]
>
> (Luke 6:27–28, 32–33.)

There is a notable array of evidence in favor of inserting in
Matthew's text at this point almost the identical wording that
is found in the additional clauses in Luke. Inasmuch as Matthew apparently had so much material at hand that he could
not use all of it in his Gospel and it became a noteworthy habit
of his to eliminate some of this material, thus shortening much
of the teaching in the parables and sayings of our Lord, it is

possible that here also he has eliminated some of the clauses
that he thought unnecessary to fill out Jesus' meaning. Luke's
version of these sayings commends itself as exhibiting the type
of parallelism and word play generally for which Jesus' poetry
was notable.

With a view to dealing with these materials as informatively
as possible, let us look first at the over-all teaching of our Lord
and then at some of the more particular details. Generally
speaking, the teaching concerns the new Christian definition of
" love." On the lips of Jesus and of those who like Paul thoroughly understood him, this word far transcended the meaning
of " love " in the world of thought and action of his day. It
transcends also the common understanding and even much of
the deeper psychological teaching of our own day regarding
" love."

It has long since become a commonplace in Biblical studies
that in the Greek the noun *agapē* — whatever may be said for
the verb associated with it — was probably an invention of the
Biblical writers. This was because the Greek words for " love "
previously employed were no longer adequate to express what
the Christian faith meant by the term. It is to be remembered,
however, that Jesus was talking in Aramaic, not in Greek — and
in Aramaic the problem just referred to does not arise. It seems
probable, as far as the evidence permits us to make a judgment
on the point, that Jesus used for " love " the words available to
him in the Aramaic of the day.[12]

The problem of what Jesus meant by the term " love," therefore, is not to be resolved on the basis of linguistics. Our approach to it must rather be that supplied by the methodology
peculiar to exegetical studies or, if one prefers, of " Biblical theology." The method employed in ascertaining the definition of
words in such scientific studies consists in an intensive study
of the word in question in its various contexts. For example, the
present context supplies us with at least two points contribu-
tory to a proper definition of the term " love " as used on the
lips of Jesus.

" Pray for your persecutors
>   That you may become sons of your Father in heaven,
>   Who makes his sun rise on evil and good,
>   Who causes his rain to fall on righteous and unright-
>   eous.
> For if you conceive love for those who love you,
>   What thanks can you expect?
>   Do not even collaborationists as much?
> And if you are on speaking terms with your ' brothers ' only,
>   Wherein are you surpassing the rest of men?
>   Do not even they as much? "

(Matt. 5:44–47.)

As will be seen, we have here, first, a suggestion of " love's " necessarily universal character. To be " love " in the sense in which Jesus uses the term, it must reflect the character of the Father in heaven, " who makes his sun rise on evil and good, who causes his rain to fall on righteous and unrighteous." This same aspect of " love " is exemplified in the parable of the good Samaritan, wherein the Samaritan is obviously the exemplary Christian who makes no distinction between men on the basis of caste, creed, color, or any other secular distinction. The point of that parable is easily overlooked by those who have not lived for an extensive period in the Orient, where a man's clothes represent a series of " badges." By a man's clothes his religion, his race, his social and economic status, and other factors may be discerned.

The point of the parable of the good Samaritan lies, then, in this, that the man was " stripped and lying naked." He had lost all his badges! And the priest and Levite, who had learned an ethic which demanded that to treat a man as one's " neighbor " or " brother " one must be able to discern these ephemeral aspects of his nature, had no other recourse in that circumstance than to " pass by on the other side." However, the Samaritan (who is the exemplary Christian) has learned that a " man's a man for a' that " and that " love " demands that one make the other man's self his own, treating him in every circumstance as one would be treated by him.

Secondly, it is obvious from the present passage that "love" on Jesus' lips is entirely devoid of thought of self. "If you conceive love for those who love you . . . Do not even collaborationists as much?" And again, "If you are on speaking terms with your Christian brothers only . . . Do not even the rest of men as much?" True "love" in Jesus' teaching has poured out thought of self in order to pour in the other's self. That the apostle Paul so understood Jesus' teaching is very clear from his description of our Lord's own action in Phil. 2:5 ff. The same teaching is found as well in the second chapter of the book of Hebrews.

One may then define "love" on Jesus' lips as follows: Love is the commitment of all one's personality (thought, feelings, and above all, will) in favor of the other's good, in spite of that other's attitude toward the one loving.

In line with this definition and the teaching more especially of this passage, it should be observed that Christian love, unlike other loves, does not choose its object. We often hear the saying: "What a prince of a fellow that chap is. I just love him!" This saying, of course, means that there is something lovable in the other which attracts my love to him. Christian love is not like this. Rather it is love of the unlovable, love in spite of the unloving and unlovable character of that other. That Paul understood this to be Jesus' meaning appears, for example, from the following: "But God commends his own love toward us in that while we were still sinners Christ died for us" (Rom. 5:8). God's love is universal and it takes all men without distinction into its universal embrace. Man's love must be no less universal. Such is Jesus' teaching.

That Jesus meant that one's love must be expressed for others regardless of their attitude toward the one loving appears from his own actions. His saying on the cross — "Father, forgive them; for they know not what they do" (Luke 23:34) — clearly embodies and transfigures his meaning at this point. The words recorded of the first Christian martyr, Stephen, indicate that he had so understood his Lord's teaching when he said, "Lord, lay not this sin to their charge" (Acts 7:60), and that he was prepared to adopt his Lord's self-abnegating spirit under the most trying circumstances.

It is at this point that Luke in his Gospel inserts the so-called "Golden Rule" which is found at Matt. 7:12. In Luke it reads: "And as you would have men do to you, do you to them likewise" (ch. 6:31). Little need be added to what has already been abundantly said by scholars as to the meaning of this maxim and the possibility that Jesus was quoting one that had already found popular acceptance.[13]

But whatever the maxim may mean on the lips of others, in the present context it certainly is clear that for Jesus it does not mean something equivalent to the "scale-pan theory" of love — a theory that suggests that on one pan of the scale one should place so much love for self and on the other an equivalent amount for the neighbor or the brother! Neither here nor elsewhere does Jesus say that one shall love the neighbor *as much as* one's self. The scale-pan theory of love takes no account of the principle of the cross. It represents, indeed, a crossless ethic! For when one places a cross on the pan that represents one's love for self, obviously the love of self is lightened and the other pan becomes correspondingly heavy! When Jesus used this maxim, therefore, he meant, not "as much as," but rather "*as*" one's self. He meant to pour out self and to pour the world in, to make the "neighbor" one's other self! In Jesus' definition of "love," therefore, the principle of the cross always is an integral element.

> "Be adults, then,
> As your Heavenly Father is of perfect stature."
> (Matt. 5:48.)

And now our Lord sums up his entire teaching on the subject of the Christian ethic with this final word. Here is a clarion call for ethical maturity, for the like of which one must turn to the Hebrew prophets of old. It recalls the teaching of those prophets that God made man in his own image and that that image alone may serve as the ethical standard of man's maturity.

C. KINGDOM RIGHTEOUSNESS AND TRUE RELIGION

Chapter X

Utter Sincerity Demanded by True Religion

Avoid doing your righteousness before men with a view to being
    seen by them,
Otherwise, you have no thanks from your Father who is in heaven.

Whenever, then, you comply with the duty respecting alms,
    Do not have a trumpet blown before you,
    As the " approval seekers " do in synagogues and market places,
    That they may be commended by men —
    I tell you truly, they get their wish!
But you — as you comply with the alms obligation,
    Do not inform your left hand of what your right is doing,
    That your almsgiving may be done in secret —
    Then it will be your Father who observes in secret
    Who will make award to you — and that openly!
Whenever, again, you are engaging in prayer,
    Do not emulate the " approval seekers,"
    Who like to stand at prayer in synagogues and at street corners,
    That they may be seen by men —
    I tell you truly, they get their wish!
But you — as you are about to pray,
    Enter your inner sanctum and close your door,
    Then pray to your Father in secret —
    And it will be your Father who observes in secret,
    Who will make award to you!
Moreover, while praying do not babble idly like the rest of men,
    Who suppose that they will be heard for their wordiness!
    Do not emulate them.
    Indeed, your Father is aware of your needs before you ask
    him. . . .

Whenever, again, you are fasting,
  Do not be glum-looking like the " approval seekers,"
  Who make their faces unsightly
  That they may appear to men to be fasting —
  I tell you truly, they get their wish!
But you — as you fast, wash your face! Anoint your head!
  That you may not appear to men to be fasting —
  Rather to your Father in secret.
  And it will be your Father who observes in secret,
  Who will make award to you.

                                        (Matt. 6:1-8, 16-18.)

We turn now to the implications of the "righteousness"
that God demands of man in the realm of religion. And as
Matt. 5:21-48, dealing with the subject of the Christian ethic,
contains Jesus' own interpretation of Beatitude Five, so the
Evangelist's sixth chapter contains our Lord's explication of the
meaning of Beatitude Six. This, it will be recalled, reads: " Privilege of those who are sincere at heart — they shall be ushered
into God's Presence! " What, then, is this *sincerity of heart*
which, as we have already seen, our Lord discovers to be a major
demand upon man in such a passage as Ps. 24:4 and to represent in some sense a reflection of God's nature as outlined in
Ps. 85:10?

In answering this question our Lord first states in Matt. 6:1
a general principle covering the total obligation of man's
reflecting God's nature among his fellows. Thereafter he presents three examples of the practical application of that principle in terms of current religious practice. The general principle he states in the words, " Avoid doing your righteousness
before men with a view to being seen by them." For " righteousness," the King James Version had " alms." This version is following an inferior type of textual tradition at this point and is
almost certainly wrong, although admittedly the evidence is
complicated.

More important for the solution of this problem than an ap-
peal to the manuscript evidence is a phenomenon to be noted
in the Syriac and Aramaic spelling of the two words " righteous-

ness" and "alms." For in these languages the two words are spelled with the same consonants, viz., " *s, d, q*." Thus, "alms" appears as *sedhqa* or *sedhqᵉtha*, and "righteousness" appears as *sadhiqu* or *sadhiqutha*. When it is recalled that in the early centuries only the consonants were written in Biblical manuscripts, it is easy to see how such a mistake could appear as that represented in the problem before us. In the Hebrew, *sedaqah* stood for both "righteousness" and "alms." And the Septuagint translators found it difficult to make a distinction between the two meanings of the word, as may be seen in the translation of Prov. 10:2 respectively in the Septuagint text and the quotation of the same verse at Tobit 4:10 and 12:9. No such confusion could possibly exist with regard to these words in the Greek, where "alms" is *eleemosune* and "righteousness" is *dikaiosune*. The confusion, therefore, is evidence of the Aramaic, doubtless in the form of a document, underlying the present passage.[1]

But, as we have already seen, "righteousness" stands for the total demand of God upon human life. It is this, then, that our Lord intends generally to be fulfilled, not in the spirit of religious exhibitionism, but rather in utter sincerity of heart, not with a view to commending one's self to men, but rather to commend one's self to God. It would seem obvious, therefore, that a general statement at the beginning of this chapter covering God's total righteous demands upon man is called for. Accordingly, the word "righteousness" is to be preferred to "alms" in the verse.

It scarcely needs mentioning, perhaps, that the teaching at this point is by no means in conflict with that at Matt. 5:16, viz.,

> "Let your light so shine out in men's view
> That they may observe your ' good works '
> And give the praise to your Father
> Who dwells in the spiritual realm."

For the motivation in the two cases is obviously quite different. The apparent contradiction is of a merely formal nature: in the

one case our Lord is commending the performance of one's
" good works " before men with a view to their bringing praise
to the Father who has inspired them; in the other case, he is
warning against the grave danger attaching to religious exhibitionism. It should be obvious that both injunctions can be
carried out at one and the same time, depending merely upon
one's motivation being right. The sincere, religious man can do
any good work before men provided always it is done, not with
the flourish of the exhibitionist, but with the sole motive of
blessing and praising God.[2]

What follows now in the remainder of our passage constitutes a series of three examples of the utter sincerity that God
demands of man in the realm of religion. These examples are
almsgiving, prayer, and *fasting.* It would be a mistake to suppose
that our Lord chooses these three examples of one's performance of religious duty in order to commend them as such. The
very words that he uses in introducing each illustration in turn
are indicative of the fact that this is not his purpose — viz.,
" Whenever, then, you comply with the duty respecting alms,"
" Whenever, again, you are engaging in prayer," and " Whenever, again, you are fasting." It is clear that he is not commending any one or all of these three forms of religious expression as though they represented something new in his teaching.
Rather, he is taking three common practices which to the religious man within contemporary Judaism constituted an acceptable mode of religious expression. His purpose, then, is to say
that if this constitutes for anyone a normative religious outlet,
he has but one thing to add, namely, that one practice it " in
spirit and in truth," with utter sincerity of heart and will.

We are, indeed, in a position to say why it was that Jesus
chose these particular modes of religious expression. During the
exile, the Israelites were " displaced persons " so far as the Temple, which was the center of their religious life in Jerusalem, was
concerned. They had been divorced from the Temple's sacrifices and festivals in a strange land. The psalmist wrote in his
extremity on such an occasion: " How shall we sing the Lord's

song in a foreign land? If I forget you, O Jerusalem, let my right hand whither! " (Ps. 137:4-5.)

In that extremity it was not only that the people of Israel were constrained to hang their lyres on the willow trees (Ps. 137:2), but they were also divorced — and this was far more serious — from the practice of Temple religion as they had previously known it. In this extremity, their religious leaders found it necessary to devise other means of religious expression.

It was no doubt out of this circumstance that the synagogue, with its prayer book and the Psalter — its hymnal — arose. Ezra (397 B.C.) is traditionally said to have been the father of the scribal movement.[3] Whether or not this tradition is historically accurate, in any case this movement which got under way shortly after the exile and was developed by the group who came to be known as the Pharisees soon became the sponsor of the synagogue with its religious and educational functions.

And the problem to which the sponsors of the synagogue addressed themselves was this: exclusive of the Temple worship with its sacrifices and rituals, what may be suggested to the common man as normative aids to true religious expression? The answer given to this problem by the scribes took the form that our Lord adopted as the outline for his own discussion as it lies before us in our passage. *Almsgiving, prayer,* and *fasting* constituted the principal expressions of true religion as taught by the Pharisees, as obviously these three could be carried on far from the Temple and throughout the known world of the day, which was practically coterminous with the Roman Empire.

Documentation of the fact that the three religious expressions referred to by our Lord in the present passage were those primarily supported by the Pharisees in the contemporary Judaism is of a voluminous nature. It will be sufficient here perhaps to make the following observations. As Simpson in his introduction to the Book of Tobit remarks, " the ' Three Pillars of Judaism,' *prayer, almsgiving, and fasting, are inculcated*" in this apocryphal work of pre-Christian Jewish piety. Similarly, Box and Oesterley suggest that " fully in accordance with these

religious views of the Pharisees are the three great watchwords
in reference to practical religion to be found in Pharisaic literature, viz., *teshubhah, w*e*thephelah, w*e*sedaqah,* i.e., repentance,
prayer, and almsgiving (lit., ' righteousness '): these three are
mentioned together as the three things which ' avert the evil
doom.' " It will be recalled that repentance and fasting are
synonymous, or rather fasting is the outer expression of repentance in the Jewish ethos — Joel 2:12 ff.[4]

A final consideration should make it appear conclusive that
Jesus is here dealing with well-known practices rather than
some which he himself wishes to sponsor. For in the passage
before us, he adopts a line of approach quite other than that
which he had employed in ch. 5. There, it will be remembered,
his every injunction began with the refrain " You have received
by tradition the saying to men of old. . . . I say to you, however." In the passage before us, on the contrary, instead of a new
injunction opposed to an old traditional saying, we read approximately the following: " When you are practicing your
alms, when you are praying, when you are fasting, I have but
one thing to add, do all with sincerity before your Father in
heaven."

> " Whenever, then, you comply with the duty respecting alms,
>   Do not have a trumpet blown before you,
>   As the ' approval seekers ' do in synagogues and mar-
>   ket places,
>   That they may be commended by men —
>   I tell you truly, they get their wish!
> *But you* — as you comply with the alms obligation,
>   Do not inform your left hand of what your right is
>   doing,
>   That your almsgiving may be done in secret —
>   Then it will be your Father who observes in secret
>   Who will make award to you — and that openly! "
>   (Matt. 6:2–4.)

Let us look now briefly at each of these three religious practices in turn. *Almsgiving* had long since been commended in the
law of Moses. Deuteronomy 14:28–29, for example, provided for

the establishment of what came to be called the "poor man's tithe." Moreover, in an agricultural community in which the harvest provided the greater part of sustenance throughout the year, the Mosaic law provided for the poor by establishing a system of gleaning in the fields and olive orchards and vineyards (Lev. 19:9 f.; 23:22; Deut. 24:19–21). In the Mishnah and Talmud the book entitled Peah ("gleanings") deals with the numerous problems involved in such a system.

In Jesus' day in consequence almsgiving was an established practice, both in the somewhat haphazard fashion practiced among all peoples of giving to beggars on the streets or at the doors of religious buildings (Acts 3:2 f.), and through organized channels such as the Temple treasury (Mark 12:41 ff.; John 8:20). M. Shekalim 5:6 states that in the Herodian Temple there was a "Chamber of Secrets," of which the remark is made that "the devout used to put their gifts in secret" in the same "and the poor of good family received support therefrom in secret."

From these and other passages in the contemporary Jewish literature, it is clear that the giving of alms for the support of the poor was considered not only a privilege but also an obligation devolving upon both rich and poor alike. George Foot Moore quotes an early passage in this literature as follows: "Almsgiving and deeds of loving-kindness are equal to all the commandments of the law. Almsgiving is exercised toward the living, deeds of loving-kindness toward the living and the dead; almsgiving to the poor, deeds of loving-kindness to the poor and to the rich; almsgiving is done with a man's money, deeds of loving-kindness either with his money or personally." In commenting upon such a passage, this author remarks: "Almsgiving itself is requited by God only in proportion to love (hesed) that there is in it. Alms given in this spirit are more than all the sacrifices (Prov. 21:3), and deeds of loving-kindness more than almsgiving (Hos. 10:12)." [5]

The Qumran sect, as the later Christian church itself (Acts 4:32–37; 5:1 ff.; 6:1–6), carried this injunction regarding alms-

giving to the logical conclusion of establishing a common fund
for the support of the community as a whole. For example, in
The Manual of Discipline we read: " All who declare their willingness to serve God's truth must bring all of their mind, all of
their strength, and all of their wealth into the community of
God." [6] The provision in what has come to be known as the
" Damascus Document" is not so severe. The relevant paragraph reads: " This is the rule for regulating public needs.
Their wages for at least two days per month are to be handed
over to the overseer. The judges are then to take thereof and
give it away for the benefit of orphans. They are also to support
therefrom the poor and needy, the aged who are dying, the persons captured by foreign peoples, unprotected girls, unmarriage-
able virgins, general communal officials." [7]

Our Lord, then, in commending the practice of almsgiving
has only one thing to say by way of addition to the common
practice of the day, viz., that one shall not give alms with a
flourish as is done by religious exhibitionists. We are not to
suppose, of course, that anyone at that time actually blew a
trumpet in order to make it appear that he was about to give
alms. Jesus is certainly speaking here, as generally, in metaphorical terms. Nor, indeed, is his suggestion that " it is the spirit
that counts " entirely new, as some of the above quotations ver-
ify. Rather, he is seeking — in line with his total teaching in the
sermon and elsewhere — to emphasize spirit as over against legalistic command and practice. Undoubtedly he does this in
opposition to, not the generality of Pharisees of his day, but
those whom he properly designates as " approval seekers," a
type of character to be found among all religious peoples and
not exclusively among Pharisees! [8]

> " Whenever, again, you are engaging in prayer,
>   Do not emulate ' approval seekers,'
>   Who like to stand at prayer in synagogues and at street
>   corners,
>   That they may be seen by men —
>   I tell you truly, they get their wish!
>   But *you* — as you are about to pray,

> Enter your inner sanctum and close your door,
> Then pray to your Father in secret —
> And it will be your Father who observes in secret,
> Who will make award to you! "
>
> (Matt. 6:5 f.)

Little need be added, to what has already been said with regard to almsgiving, in the matter of the other two aspects of the
current Jewish religious practice — viz., prayer and fasting. That
the need for *prayer* — both public and private — was one of the
major emphases of current Pharisaism needs scarcely to be doc-
umented. It speaks for itself that, in addition to the Greek word
synogoge being used for the Jewish house of worship, that of
proseuche (i.e., " prayer ") was also in use (Acts 16:16). Whatever Aramaic may be supposed to stand behind the Greek at
this point, it becomes clear that the major stress in any descrip-
tive term for the synagogue is that it is " a house of prayer." [9]

As for the right attitude in prayer, M. Berakoth has much to
say on this point, some of which is quite in line with Jesus' in-
culcation of a right spirit of utter sincerity. It is true that the
Pharisaic Jew in those days, like the modern Moslem, prayed
with his face toward the Holy City and wherever he might be —
whether in field or market place, on the road or in the secret
chamber of his own home. Nonetheless, that all this was by no
means done for the sake of exhibitionism appears from an abundance of quotations, among them the following:

> " None may stand up to say the Tefillah [the daily prayer of
> eighteen benedictions] save in sober mood. The pious men
> of old used to wait an hour before they said the Tefillah, that
> they might direct their heart toward God. Even if the king sa-
> lutes a man, he may not return the greeting; and even if a
> snake was twisted around his heel, he may not interrupt his
> prayer."

> " If he was riding on an ass, he should dismount [to say the
> Tefillah]. If he cannot dismount, he should turn his face [to-
> ward Jerusalem]; and if he cannot turn his face, he should di-
> rect his heart toward the Holy of Holies."
>
> (M. Berakoth 5:1 and 4:5.)

> " Moreover, while praying do not babble idly like the rest of
>   men,
>   Who suppose that they will be heard for their wordi-
>   ness!
>   Do not emulate them.
>   Indeed, your Father is aware of your needs before you
>   ask him."

(Matt. 6:16.)

As for Jesus' suggestion that his disciples should " not babble
idly like the rest of men," Matthew Black has made the interesting, and to my mind conclusive, suggestion that " there is
scarcely need for Jews to be exhorted not to pray as *Gentiles,*
as we read in the usual translations." He believes, therefore,
that the expression of the Greek stands for the Aramaic *sharka
de'enasha,* which has the meaning indicated in the text (" the
rest of men ").[10] If this suggestion is accepted, then Jesus will
here be comparing his disciples (and their practice at prayer) to
those from among both Jews and Gentiles who are unlearned in
the proper attitude inculcated by his teaching. It is these disciples who know indeed that their Father is aware of their needs
before they ask him.

> " Whenever, again, you are fasting,
>   Do not be glum-looking like the ' approval seekers,'
>   Who make their faces unsightly
>   That they may appear to men to be fasting —
>   I tell you truly, they get their wish!
>   But *you* — as you fast, wash your face! Anoint your head!
>   That you may not appear to men to be fasting —
>   Rather to your Father in secret.
>   And it will be your Father who observes in secret,
>   Who will make award to you."

(Matt. 6:17–18.)

Fasting, too, was a common practice with the Pharisees and
those who learned at their feet. It is true that no specific passage
in the Mosaic law could be cited for the necessity of either public or private fasts. The nearest approach, it seems, to an injunction for men to fast is found in Lev. 16:29, where the reference

is to one's attitude on the Day of Atonement: " And it shall be a statute to you for ever that in the seventh month, on the tenth day of the month, *you shall afflict yourselves*." There is, however, abundant evidence from the Old Testament itself that the patriarchs and prophets and their disciples did fast. (Judg. 20:26; I Sam. 7:6; Ezra 8:23; Zech. 7:5; Ps. 35:13; and the like.) The practice also was common in Jesus' day, as reference to such passages as the following clearly indicates: Mark 2:18; Luke 18:12; Acts 10:30. Our Lord himself fasted (Matt. 4:2). As for the Pharisees, it was their custom to observe fasting on Mondays and Thursdays of each week (M. Taanith 1:6). Moreover, the book of the Mishnah just cited was written with a view to indicating the nature and length of fasting to be observed when the harvest rains failed.

The curious passage in the Didache 8:1 — " Let not your fast be with the hypocrites, for they fast on Mondays and Thursdays, but do you fast on Wednesdays and Fridays " — indicates what a legalistic attitude within the Christian church itself could make of this subject of fasting. Once again, however, our Lord's teaching is with a view to inculcating a right spirit in this as in all religious observances.

Some years ago Adolf Deissmann pointed out that the Greek word (*epechein*) translated here " they get their wish " is one which in the Greek papyri turning up in the sands of Egypt is used in connection with receipts. Before one signs his name to such a document he adds *epechein* to express what in English we should indicate by the words " received payment in full." It is unlikely that this dramatic application of the verb can be borne out in the underlying Aramaic. However, it certainly does express Jesus' attitude to the whole subject of religious exhibitionism. It is true, in fact, that religious exhibitionists can always secure a following. Our Lord's meaning, then, is that when such a following has been secured, inasmuch as that is the religious exhibitionist's desire, he should, so to speak, sign a receipt — " received payment in full "! What more can such an exhibitionist expect?

There is, however, abundant evidence that in the matter of rewards Jesus' teaching was not that one may expect a *quid pro quo* or a tit for tat in his dealings with God. This is certainly a major point in the parable of the workers in the vineyard (Matt. 20:1–16) and in that of the unprofitable servant (Luke 17:7–10). There are rewards held out to the Christian disciple, but these are rewards of grace in Jesus' teachings even as for Paul and the rest of the New Testament, as we shall see more exactly when we study the seventh chapter of the Sermon.

Chapter XI

The Lord's Prayer

As for you, *then, pray in this manner* —
  " *Our Father in heaven:*
      Thy name — *be it hallowed,*
      Thy Kingdom — *may it come,*
      Thy will — *be it done,*
      On earth as in heaven.
  Give us our bread day by day.
  Forgive us our debts
      As we, too, forgive our debtors; —
  Do not lead us into temptation,
      But deliver us from the Evil One."
For if you shall forgive men their trespasses, —
Your Heavenly Father also will forgive you:
But if you shall not forgive men, —
Your Father will not forgive your trespasses.

(Matt. 6:9–15.)

In this chapter we are to study the well-known prayer commonly called " The Lord's Prayer." We have isolated it from its context, that the three religious modes of expression might be treated separately in the previous chapter and to reserve the present chapter for the study of the prayer by itself.

Before discussing its teaching, it will be well to look at two questions of an introductory nature. These concern, first, the time and place assigned to the prayer by Matthew and Luke, together with the associated question of its content and length; and secondly, its relation to the Tefillah, or daily prayer recited from time immemorial by the pious Jew.

As for the first of these problems, it is well known that the so-called Lord's Prayer is found in two forms — that of Matthew in the present passage and that at Luke 11:2–4. Moreover, in the two Gospels the prayer is found in two differing situations — in the Sermon on the Mount with Matthew, and in Luke at an indeterminate point after Jesus is said to have left Galilee to "set his face to go to Jerusalem" (Luke 9:51), after, too, he has been with Mary and Martha in the village of Bethany (Luke 10:38–42).

From the reference in Mark 11:25 f. with regard to "the remission of sins," together with the late appearance of the prayer with the like teaching in Luke, ch. 11, Lagrange argues that Luke found the Lord's Prayer lying relatively late in the sources available to him. If this suggestion of Lagrange is adopted, it might even be argued that the Lord's Prayer was taught his disciples by Jesus as late as Passion Week. But as Lagrange suggests, there is no reason why Jesus may not have uttered the prayer in both contexts and in two different ways. In any case there is no great difference between the teaching involved in the two forms, Matthew's tradition merely making explicit at certain points what is already in Luke's.[1] But as both Lagrange and T. W. Manson remark, "the form in Matthew early became the form for liturgical use in the church."[2] Perhaps the earliest certain proof of this statement occurs in the Didache 8:2 f., which suggests the use of the prayer in Matthew's form toward the close of the first or the beginning of the second century in the liturgy of the church.

The related question of the length and content of the prayer in the two traditions is possibly solved by the suggestion that our Lord may have taught it in two forms to his disciples. There can be no question, however, that the liturgical use of the prayer in the early church led to modification, harmonization between the two traditions, and the addition of a liturgical ending. We shall discuss these problems briefly as we look at the several parts of the prayer itself.

Regarding the second problem — that, namely, of the relation

of the Lord's Prayer to the daily prayer employed by Jews
(Tefillah or Shemoneh Esreh) — all that may be said at the moment must be unfortunately of a relatively inconclusive nature.
This prayer, which is made up of eighteen benedictions or
ascriptions of praise, is the formal prayer recited thrice a day by
the pious Jew through the centuries. This prayer has had a long
history and various additions have been made to it from time to
time.[3]

That there are ascriptions of praise in the Tefillah, as in other
well-known Jewish prayers, which are similar to or even identical with those in the Lord's Prayer, is unquestionable.[4] But to
conclude from such chance similarities that " Jesus presented
the Lord's Prayer in conscious opposition to the portions of the
Shemoneh Esreh current in his time, with a view to supplanting
it in the circle of his disciples is," as Strack-Billerbeck rightly
conclude, " incapable of demonstration." [5] For we have no
knowledge how far the Shemoneh Esreh was used in private
prayer at the time, nor does a study of the two prayers in conjunction suggest any conscious opposition of the one to the
other.

A careful study of the prayer itself, indeed, suggests rather
that this is not a formula of prayer at all in Jesus' original intention. The church, it is true, made it from the very beginning
a part of its liturgy and, as we shall see, for that purpose rounded
it out with a liturgical ending. But in its original intent it appears to be rather teaching about the nature of prayer than a
form of prayer to be recited day by day.

As has often been observed, the Lord's Prayer, like the Ten
Commandments, divides itself naturally into two parts. As
found in the Matthean form before us, the first part consists
of vs. 9 and 10, and the second part similarly of vs. 11 to 13. In
both commandments and prayer the first part deals with man's
attitude toward God, his first obligation (Ex. 20:1–11). Similarly, the second part of both passages deals with man's duty to
his fellow man (Ex. 20:12–17). This twofold division accords
well with the entire teaching of Scripture, which, as Karl Barth

pointed out a number of years ago, enjoins upon man two du-
ties — a vertical one toward God and a horizontal one toward
his fellow man. It also accords with our Lord's teaching regarding the two commandments of first importance at Mark 12:29–
31.[6]

On closer inspection, however, the second paragraph of the
prayer is seen to have a wider reference than that indicated in
the commandments. Indeed, not only man's social attitudes, but
all his physical and spiritual needs are briefly brought into focus
in this part of the prayer. It thus becomes possible to observe
that by teaching the prayer in this form, our Lord intends to
suggest that, once the praying man has committed his will to
the will of God, he may pray for any of his needs. Such teaching is, of course, in line with our Lord's own example, as seen
for instance in his experience in the Garden of Gethsemane,
where he prayed, "Abba, Father, all things are possible to thee;
remove this cup from me; yet not what I will, but what thou
wilt" (Mark 14:36). The like thought, of course, occurs in a
number of passages in John's Gospel, as for example, "For I
have come down from heaven, not to do my own will, but the
will of him who sent me" (John 6:38; see ch. 18:11).

From the foregoing observations, we conclude that by means
of this model prayer our Lord would teach the comprehensive
nature of God's interest in man and at the same time his requirement that man manifest an integrated series of responses
to that comprehensive interest. It is only as man recognizes the
supremacy of God's will and sovereignty over his life, that man
may pray for anything. But having duly recognized that will and
that sovereignty, he may pray for all of his individual and social
needs!

> " *As for you*, then, pray in this manner —
> ' Our Father in heaven:
>   Thy name — be it hallowed,
>   Thy Kingdom — may it come,
>   Thy will — be it done,
>   On earth as in heaven.' "

(Matt. 6:9 f.)

Looking now at the first part of the prayer, we observe at the very start a significant difference between its two forms as it lies in the Gospels. Matthew reads, "Our Father in heaven," whereas Luke has merely the one word of address, "Father" (Luke 11:2). Of these two traditions, probably that of Luke is the more original. It seems to have been the custom within the contemporary Jewish ethos to address God in the Matthean form, and it is likely that Matthew therefore places the common form on the lips of Jesus.[7]

On the other hand, the Gospels seem to make it clear that Jesus used the simpler form, "Father," in his own practice of prayer (Mark 14:36; Luke 10:21; 23:46). This simple form appeared in the Aramaic which Jesus spoke as *abba* (transliterated in Mark 14:36) and was taken over by the early Palestinian church, as appears clear from Paul's writings (Rom. 8:15; Gal. 4:6).[8] J. M. Creed has made the valuable observation that the repetition of the word for "Father" in some of these passages in Aramaic and Greek "may carry us back to the earliest church at Jerusalem, when Aramaic-speaking and Greek-speaking congregations of believers worshiped side by side."[9] From all these considerations we are led to conclude that Jesus taught his disciples in addressing God merely to say, "Father." It was, then, the wish on Matthew's part to phrase the prayer's opening in the form to which his Jewish Christian readers had been accustomed that gave rise to the salutation, "Our Father in heaven." And it was no doubt the same motivation that led later scribes to harmonize the Lucan address with the Matthean.

There follow now three petitions in parallel form that the "name," "Kingdom," and "will" of God shall be acknowledged "on earth as in heaven." These three petitions represent the sort of synonymous parallelism to which we have previously referred as being characteristic of Semitic poetry generally. And as is true of such parallelism elsewhere, the three petitions essentially stand for one request, but not quite. That is to say, while generally synonymous, they severally represent variations upon one theme. This theme is the prophetic doctrine of the

Sovereignty of God. This Sovereignty or Lordship attaches, of course, to God's *person*, for which in true Semitic fashion the "name" always stands.[10] Again, God's Lordship finds expression in the coming of his "Kingdom" into the world. And finally, his Sovereignty is realized as his "will" is done.

That these three petitions do stand for essentially the same thing is rather significantly indicated by the absence of one or more of them in the parallel passage in Luke. There, only the first of the petitions — "Thy name be hallowed" — has an undisputed place in the various manuscripts and versions. Marcion had a traditional form of the Lord's Prayer which contained a petition for the coming of the Holy Spirit, rather than of the Kingdom, upon his disciples. And most of the manuscripts and versions in Luke omitted the third petition, together with the closing phrase "on earth as in heaven." There is, of course, no reason why our Lord may not have taught this portion of the prayer to his disciples in both the shorter form in Luke and the longer as in Matthew. In any case, the parallel poetic structure in Matthew commends itself as certainly original with our Lord, though the shorter form as in Luke was sufficient to express his meaning.

Much controversy has been expended as to the exact sense in which Jesus meant the petition about the Kingdom's coming to be taken. When, however, it is observed that the three clauses have to do with the one idea of the implementation of God's Lordship, and moreover that this is to be done "on earth as in heaven," it appears inevitable that this petition must be understood in the most comprehensive way. The Hebrew and Greek words that are ordinarily translated "kingdom," as these pertain to God's rule among men, have behind them a long history. They stand both for the abstract idea of "lordship" or "sovereignty" and also for the concrete expression of the same on the plane of human history. This concrete expression, moreover, takes the form of both *individual* and *corporate* commitment to God's rule over men's lives, as this is expressed in the formation of a "people of God," on the one hand, and the acceptance on the part of every member of that people of God's Lordship over their lives, on the other. This concretizing of the concept of the divine Sovereignty obviously has no end right down to the end of history itself and to the final consummation of the Kingdom when God shall be all in all.[11]

In view of these facts, when our Lord asks his disciples to pray for the coming of the Kingdom of God, certainly we must understand this petition in the most comprehensive sense, as has just been remarked. *God's Kingdom comes* when the individual accepts his rule over that individual's life — a fact dramatized by the Jewish synagogue throughout the centuries in the recitation of the Shema. (M. Berakoth 2:2 and Mark 10:15.) *God's Kingdom comes* as well in the fellowship of the " people of God " and it finds realization on the plane of history in the corporate experience of the church of Christ, in so far as that church constitutes the very " body of Christ " and so forms the active instrument for the doing of its Lord's will in the world. Finally, *God's Kingdom comes* at the end of history when God will be " all in all " (I Cor. 15:28).

> " Give us our bread day by day.
> Forgive us our debts
> As we, too, forgive our debtors;
> Do not lead us into temptation,
> But deliver us from the Evil One."
> (Matt. 6:11–13.)

We turn now to the second part of the prayer, relating to man in all of his individual and social needs. Let it be remarked at once that the comprehensive character of this portion of the prayer makes it plain that in Jesus' teaching, once man had committed himself to the Lordship of God over his life, he might pray for anything required in any department thereof. This is because God is interested in all of human living and not only in any one segment of the same. Man's life is considered by Jesus as a unit as is the case throughout the Scriptures generally. It is not compartmentalized so as to suggest that God is interested in only moral or spiritual, and not as well in physical and material, needs.

This portion of the prayer, therefore, begins with the lower material wants. At once we are confronted with a difficulty. What is meant by the Greek ordinarily translated " give us this day our daily bread," or " our bread for the morrow," or " our super-substantial bread," or " the bread of our need," and the like? Such possible renderings are found in the Syriac and Latin as well as in the English versions. One imagines that Matthew Black has given us the final solution to this problem when he suggests that the words usually rendered " this day " and " daily " represent a misunderstanding of the underlying Aramaic in which our Lord was speaking. That Aramaic meant " day by day " and was correctly reproduced in the Greek rendered " each day " in the parallel passage at Luke 11:3. A literal translation of the Aramaic would be " today and tomorrow " as found at Luke 13:32, or as in the Hebrew at Ex. 19:10 and Hos. 6:2. The translation given above — " give us our bread day by day " — is that of Matthew Black.[12]

The purpose of Jesus, then, in teaching his disciples to pray for their bread day by day was at once to suggest to their minds a sense of constant dependence upon God for all the needs of life and again to assert his interest in all those needs whatever they might be. The suggestion sometimes made that our Lord enjoined prayer for only the necessities of life represents a total misunderstanding of the Oriental use of the word " bread " in a passage like the present. In the so-called " wheat crescent " extending from the Levant to Northern India, bread is the staple article of diet just as beef was in medieval England. The King James Version, therefore, properly translated the Greek " bread " to read " meat." Both " bread " and " meat," therefore, in the contexts in which they were respectively used, may very well stand for a seven-course dinner! God does not keep his people on a starvation diet!

" Forgive us our debts as we, too, forgive our debtors." The Judaism of Jesus' day conceived of sin in terms of debt, or of an obligation owed to God. This point of view was in part at least the product of the prophetic doctrine of the Sovereignty of God, which dramatized the relationship between God and man in terms of that of lord to slave or of creditor to debtor. That Jesus accepted this point of view appears from several of his parables, as for example that of the unrighteous steward in Matt. 18:21–35 and of the unprofitable servant at Luke 17:7–10. The same teaching is found in Jesus' parable of the two debtors which he uttered in the presence of Simon the Pharisee on the occasion of the feet-washing incident (Luke 7:36–50). In such a context "sins" represent unfulfilled obligations which man "owes" to God.

The thought contained in this petition that God forgives only those of a forgiving spirit must have been a major teaching of our Lord. It is found again in vs. 14 and 15 below, as well as at Mark 11:25: "And whenever you stand praying, forgive, if you have anything against any one; so that your Father also who is in heaven may forgive you your trespasses." And as we have already seen in the Sermon (Matt. 5:23 f.), reconciliation with God is not to be expected apart from reconciliation with one's brother. There are rabbinic parallels to this teaching of our Lord. But what is more to the point, his teaching here accords with one of the deeper insights of modern psychology to the effect that forgiveness can be realized only by a person who has himself a spirit of forgiveness. The usual translation — "as we also have forgiven our debtors" — represents a mistaken interpretation of both the Greek and the Aramaic. Jesus is not saying that his disciples must forgive *before* they may expect God's forgiveness. As Joüon remarks, "we forgive at the very moment (of our prayer for forgiveness); the action (i.e., our forgiveness) is accomplished at the very moment when one speaks. This is the sense of the *aorist aphekamen*, which corresponds to the Aramaic perfect." Both the Greek aorist and the Aramaic perfect, therefore, should be translated by the English present as we have done above: "Forgive us our debts as we, too, forgive our debtors." [13]

"Do not lead us into temptation, but deliver us from the Evil One." One cannot but feel that much nonsense has been spoken and written about this petition of the prayer. It is often suggested that there is no need of praying that God should not lead us into temptation, as, of course, he would never do such a thing. Would he not? Matthew 4:1 is very good evidence that he did just that to his Son: "Then Jesus was led up by the Spirit into the wilderness to be tempted by the Devil." The desire to see one tempted may always have behind it one or other of two motivations — an evil one that thereby the tempted may fall, or a good one that thereby the tempted may become stronger morally and spiritually. The eagle pushes her young out of the nest and then swoops down to catch the fledgling before disaster befalls. The wise parent will lead his child into a situation of danger that through the testing the knowledge of that danger may be discovered. So it is with God. The petition before us, therefore, is one intended to teach the danger of spiritual arrogance. "Let no man," it seems to say, "think himself so strong that he may enter into temptation with a proud spirit. Rather, realizing his own inadequacy, let him remind God of his weakness and petition his Father not to permit him to be tempted even for his own good! So let him learn and give expression to a spirit of utter dependence upon that God who allows temptation to come in human experience."

The positive opposite of the last petition is its counterpart — "but deliver us from the Evil One." The Greek here permits of our translating by either the abstract or the concrete term, that is, by either "evil" or "the Evil One." But Jesus was speaking of those who believed in the existence of some sort of personification of all the evil forces to be found in God's world. This personification was variously spoken of as the Devil, Satan, Mastema, Belial, Beelzebub, and the like. These terms all stand for that corporate sin of the race which Saint Augustine termed "original sin." Such evil lies around us men on every hand, and it is with the spiritual forces of darkness which it represents that our moral warfare is carried on (Eph. 6:10–20).[14]

The liturgical ending that we employ in rounding out the Lord's Prayer for purposes of public worship comes almost verbatim from I Chron. 29:11–13, wherein David blesses his people, " the people of God," shortly before his death. It is found in varying forms in the Greek manuscripts and versions, the oldest single witness to it being perhaps the Didache, in which it reads " for thine is the power and the glory forever." It was undoubtedy added by the church for liturgical purposes near the beginning of the second Christian century. It is appropriately used, therefore, in our liturgies but finds no part in the teaching of Jesus. It is, however, thoroughly in his spirit and in accord with his teaching generally.

Chapter XII

Utter Consecration to the Right God

Do not treasure to yourselves treasures on earth,
    Where moth and decay disfigure
    And where thieves force an entrance and steal:
But treasure to yourselves treasures in heaven,
    Where neither moth nor decay disfigure
    And where thieves neither force an entrance nor steal:
For where your treasure is, there your heart will be also.

The eye is the body's lamp.
    If, then, your eye be clear, your whole body will be alight;
    But if your eye be clouded, your whole body will be darkened.
    If, then, the light in you is darkness, how great that darkness!
No one can serve two lords:
    Either he will hate the one and love the other,
    Or he will endure the one and despise the other.
    You cannot serve God and mammon.
Wherefore, I say to you,
    " Cease being anxious for your life — what you shall eat;
    For your body — what you shall wear."
    Is not life more than food
    And the body than clothing?
Look at the birds of the heavens
    Which neither sow nor reap nor store:
    Your Heavenly Father nourishes them —
    Are you not more important than they?
    In any case, which of you (by anxiety) can add to his stature a
        cubit?
Again, why worry about clothing?
Consider the wild country lilies — how they grow!
    They neither labor nor spin!

But I tell you, " Solomon with all his splendor
Was not garbed like one of them! "
But if God so clothes a wild country reed —
   One that exists today
   And tomorrow is cast into an oven —
Will he not much more you, O " little-faith " ones?
Then, be not anxious, saying,
   " What are we to eat?
   What are we to drink?
   What are we to wear? "
For it is for all these that the rest of men seek:
For your Heavenly Father is aware that you need all these.

But as for you, seek first the Kingdom of God and his righteousness,
And all these will be added for you.

Then be not anxious for the morrow,
For the morrow will be anxious on its own:
Sufficient for a day is its own evil!

(Matt. 6:19–34.)

We return now to the problem of right attitudes in the realm of religion. As we have already observed in Chapter X, the first attitude that God's righteous demand places upon man in this realm is one of *utter sincerity*. It is, however, possible to be at once utterly sincere and at the same time " dead wrong "! Certainly one must grant that earnest and sincere men and women are found holding wrong philosophies of life at every level of experience — the political, the economic, the social, and the like. It is to be expected, too, that sincere people are committed to all sorts of religious belief and practice. In consequence, in addition to utter sincerity, true religion equally demands *utter consecration to the right God*.

Essentially, it is this matter of consecration to God and his purposes for human life that is the subject of Jesus' teaching in the passage before us. That this is so is apparent from the summary of the teaching at v. 33 — " But as for you, seek first the Kingdom of God and his righteousness, and all these will be added for you." The clause that closes v. 24 — " You cannot serve God and mammon " — may also serve as the theme of the passage as a whole. Here as elsewhere in his teachings, our Lord would stress the necessity of his disciples' making a choice between the great spiritual values, on the one hand, and those of an evanescent nature which are dear to the secular world, on the other.

Unlike most of the passage under discussion in Chapter X (ch. 6:1–8, 16–18), the passage before us has drawn almost entirely from the source common to Matthew and Luke ("Q"). In Luke's Gospel this material is found in three separate chapters: at chs. 11:34–36; 12:22–34; and 16:13. Matthew's verse 34 is the only complete verse in the passage that has no corresponding parallel in Luke's Gospel. Whether on the one hand Matthew rearranged his "Q" material at this point, piecing together certain sayings that our Lord uttered in the various contexts given in Luke, or, on the other, Jesus himself may have used the material on more than one occasion and grouped it after various fashions (two of which are preserved in Matthew and Luke), is still a moot question among scholars. We shall not endeavor here to decide the question but shall discuss the passage as it stands in Matthew's order.

The following short synopsis of the teaching of the passage as a whole is offered with a view to aiding the general reader to grasp quickly the nature of our Lord's teaching. (1) He introduces his argument with a statement, clothed in parabolic fashion as was his custom, to the effect that spiritual values ("treasures in heaven") are to be distinguished from secular ones ("treasures on earth"). Moreover, he makes it clear at this point that men are called upon to make a decision for which of these values they will strive (vs. 19–21; see Luke 12:33 f.). (2) This challenge is followed by a statement, again in parabolic form, to the effect that spiritual insight is required to discern where the true values of life reside. Such spiritual insight, he says, may or may not be clearly possessed by the individual (vs. 22 f.; see Luke 11:34–36). (3) Following this suggestion regarding the need for spiritual insight, the challenge is repeated to his disciples to make a choice between the two values involved, and this time it concludes with the clear statement, "You cannot serve God and mammon" (v. 24; Luke 16:13).

(4) There now follows a series of aphorisms and metaphors intended to indicate, for those who have the key to such parabolic language, what constitute the spiritual values on the one hand and the evanescent, secular ones on the other. Here our Lord distinguishes the spiritual values as "life" and "body" and the evanescent values as "food" and "clothing" (v. 25)! (5) There now follow two poetical and parabolic illustrations: the first dealing with the "birds of the heavens" to show that God cares for his creatures and supplies them with "food" (vs. 26 f.); the second referring to the "wild country lilies" with a view to showing equally that God provides "clothing" for his creatures (vs. 28–30). (6) These illustrations are now followed by an exhortation against anxiety with regard to: "What are we to eat? What are we to drink? What are we to wear?" "The rest of men seek" after these things but Jesus' disciples are not to do so (vs. 31 f.). (7) The entire passage now ends with the exhortation that Jesus' disciples are to "seek first the Kingdom of God and his righteousness," assured that "all these will be added for you" (v. 33). This section definitive of the spiritual and material values is paralleled in Luke 12: 22–31.

(8) There follows, then, in Matthew what appears like an anticlimax (and with no parallel in Luke): "Then be not anxious for the morrow, for the morrow will be anxious on its own: Sufficient for a day is its own evil!" (Matt. 6:34).

"Do not treasure to yourselves treasures on earth,
    Where moth and decay disfigure
    And where thieves force an entrance and steal:
But treasure to yourselves treasures in heaven,
    Where neither moth nor decay disfigure
    And where thieves neither force an entrance nor steal:
For where your treasure is, there your heart will be also."
                                        (Matt. 6:19–21.)

The entire passage before us, like the rest of the Sermon, was undoubtedly cast by our Lord in poetical form. By way of illustrating the parallelism and rhythm which no doubt was found throughout this whole passage, I venture herewith to quote two of the lines of the opening paragraph, together with Matthew Black's retranslation of the same into what may well have been the original Aramaic, as follows:

> "Do not treasure to yourselves treasures on earth, . . .
>   (*la th*^{e}*simun l*^{e}*naphsh* ^{e}*khon simatha b*^{e}'*ar'a*)
> But treasure to yourselves treasures in heaven . . .
>   (*simu l*^{e}*naphsh*^{e}*khon simatha bish*^{e}*mayya*)."

Even the reader unacquainted with Aramaic, one imagines, can discern the alliteration and rhythm to be found in a couplet of this sort.[1]

This contrasting of the "treasures on earth" with the "treasures in heaven" on Jesus' part reminds one strongly of the argument in The Letter to the Hebrews, where the earthly tabernacle, its sacrifices, its furnishings, and its high priest are constantly placed in contrast with the like appurtenances of the true tabernacle which is said to be in heaven (Heb. 8:4; 9:24; 10:34; etc.). The Fourth Gospel has the like contrast at ch. 3:12 — "If I have told you earthly things and you do not believe, how can you believe if I tell you heavenly things?" Similarly, at ch. 3:31 — "He who is of the earth belongs to the earth, and of the earth he speaks; he who comes from heaven is above all." Paul also was familiar with this sort of comparison, as appears in I Cor. 15:40 — "There are celestial bodies and there are terrestrial bodies; but the glory of the celestial is one, and the glory of the terrestrial is another" (see also vs. 47 ff.). He has the same contrast in mind in Phil. 3:19 f. — "with minds set on earthly things. But our commonwealth is in heaven." (See also James 3:15; I Peter 1:4.)

This contrast between the moral and spiritual values, on the one hand, and the material or transitory ones, on the other, had long been a familiar one to the Jewish mind. It is not to be understood along the lines of Platonic thought as though the earthly values were to be equated with the "unreal" and the heavenly with the "real." Neither the Hebrew prophets nor the Judaism contemporary with Jesus' day thought in such terms. Moreover, there is no evidence that Jesus was at any point Platonic in his thinking.

Yet it seems equally certain that Jesus could speak in terms such as are used here and be readily understood by his Jewish disciples. There is a famous passage in the Mishnah at Peah 1:1 which reads, "These are things for which no measure is prescribed." And then after mentioning several, it sums them up as "deeds of loving-kindness and the study of the law. These are things whose fruits a man enjoys in this world while the capital is laid up for him in the world to come: honoring father and mother, deeds of loving-kindness, making peace between a man and his fellow; and the study of the law is equal to them all." No doubt the rabbi responsible for such a saying as this would have been surprised beyond measure to have been told that the "fruits" that he enjoyed "in this world" were not equally *real* with the "capital" which he said pertained to the "world to come."

Similarly, our Lord here is not contrasting "treasures on earth" as though they were *unreal* with "treasures in heaven" as being *real!* The Platonic distinction between *real* and *unreal* does not arise in Jesus' teaching. His teaching represents rather a parabolic manner of speech which we translate adequately into our modern vernacular when we contrast the material values with moral and spiritual ones, realizing that both may be enjoyed within the framework of time and space in which we now live our lives. Our Lord's warning, therefore, is directed against that attitude of the secular world which finds its ultimate values in transitory, material ones. Moral and spiritual values, appreciated and enjoyed in this life, are for him the abiding ones and it is in these that we are to find our deepest satisfaction. One imagines that our Lord's disciple Paul, in this as in so many other ways, had penetrated to the heart of his

Lord's teaching when he declared: "For I have learned, in whatever state I am, to be content. I know how to be abased, and I know how to abound; in any and all circumstances I have learned the secret of facing plenty and hunger, abundance and want" (Phil. 4:11f.).[2]

The motivation behind such teaching as our Lord is giving here is that expressed in the final clause of this paragraph: "For where your treasure is, there your heart will be also" (v. 21). In our modern speech we speak of "a right sense of values," of the necessity of "putting first things first," of "getting things in proper focus," of "finding a single goal for one's life," of "the unified personality," and the like. It is undoubtedly of this subject that our Lord is speaking in his own parabolic way.

> "The eye is the body's lamp.
>> If, then, your eye be clear, your whole body will be alight;
>> But if your eye be clouded, your whole body will be darkened.
>> If, then, the light in you is darkness, how great that darkness!"

(Matt. 6:22 f.)

Quite naturally now our Lord speaks of the need of right moral and spiritual insight to discover wherein the higher values of life reside. And in our judgment this paragraph fits in better in the Matthean context than in that at Luke 11:34-36. In Matthew's vs. 25-34 below he is to draw the contrast between the eternal personality factors of "life" and "body" and their transitory needs of "food" and "clothing." In consequence, in the present paragraph when he speaks of the body's "eye," it should be obvious that he has in mind, not the physical eye, but rather the eternal or spiritual "eye" which belongs to the eternal "body." Unfortunately, the contrast between the right and wrong sort of spiritual insight intended by our Lord is not well expressed in the Greek text as we have it. That text contrasts the "single" eye with the "evil" or "sickly" eye. It is not at once apparent in what sense the adjective "single" is used in this connection. Our Lord's Aramaic lying behind the Greek text must have expressed some such ideas as those indicated by our adjectives "clear" and "clouded." [3]

It should be noticed in passing that this contrast between "light" and "darkness" recalls much of our Lord's teaching in the Gospel of John. In that Gospel he speaks of walking in "the light," on the one hand, and in "the darkness," on the other (John 11:10 f.); of the light shining in the darkness (ch. 1:5); and of being children of light (ch. 12:36; see I John 1:7; 2:9 f.). Similarly, the Johannine literature has much to say about "darkness" and those who love the darkness rather than the light (John 1:5; 3:19; 8:12; 12:35, 46; see I John 1:5 f.; 2:8 ff.). One is reminded also of the contemporary writings of the Qumran sect, particularly that entitled "The War of the Sons of Light and the Sons of Darkness" — writings that make it clear that such contrast between "light" and "darkness" would readily be understood by Jesus' Palestinian audience.

> "No one can serve two lords:
>> Either he will hate the one and love the other,
>> Or he will endure the one and despise the other.
>> You cannot serve God and mammon."
>>> (Matt. 6:24.)

The challenge to choose between "two lords," that is, between "God and mammon," which now follows in Matthew, is found in a different context in Luke at ch. 16:13. There the context is one of faithfulness in little and in much (vs. 10–12), or if one accepts the larger context to be found in vs. 1–9, then in that of the parable of the unrighteous steward. The present context in the Matthean account, however, is certainly equally valid. For the earthly treasures may well be summed up or even personified under the name of "mammon," which has good standing in the contemporary Aramaic as a word meaning "profit," "money," or "wealth." [4]

That our Lord set wealth and God over against one another

as opposing claimants upon the loyalty of his disciples is clear
from numerous passages in his teachings. In the story of the
young ruler (Luke 18:18–25), after a brief but comprehensive survey of the young man's life, Jesus brings him up short
with the realization that at the point of major decision he has
chosen to give his highest allegiance to the evanescent things
in life rather than to God. The antithesis is stated again in the
parable of the rich man and Lazarus (Luke 16:19–31): the
center of life for the rich man was his wealth. Having chosen
self-satisfaction as his goal, he is incapable of the spiritual insight needed to discern both the vertical and horizontal demands of true religion. Still another challenge to choose is
seen in the parable of the rich fool (Luke 12:16–21), in which
Jesus portrays a man whose wealth itself predisposes him to
think of life's problems as capable of material solutions. In his
case the setting up of a sort of ancient surplus commodity
corporation is given as evidence that he has failed to take God
into account.

There is, however, no element of asceticism in Jesus' teaching, such as that which we find in the monastic order represented at the contemporary Khirbet Qumran. Otherwise, he
could never have made the sort of statement that he did in
connection with the criticism leveled at him and at John the
Baptist, respectively, by his contemporaries: " The Son of man
has come eating and drinking; and you say, ' Behold, a glutton
and a drunkard, a friend of tax collectors and sinners !' " (Luke
7:34).

But, though not an ascetic, Jesus' teaching on the subject
of wealth is certainly as drastic as that of I Tim. 6:10 (" Love
of money is the root of every form of evil "). Jesus' suggestion
that God and mammon stand over against one another as two
lords claiming man's utmost allegiance is not to be lightly
taken. This challenge in his day had the prophetic ring about
it like that presented by Joshua to Israel when they were about
to enter the Promised Land: " And if you be unwilling to serve
the Lord, choose this day whom you will serve, whether the

gods your fathers served in the region beyond the River, or the
gods of the Amorites in whose land you dwell; but as for me
and my house, we will serve the Lord" (Josh. 24:15; see also
I Kings 18:21).

> "Wherefore, I say to you,
>   ' Cease being anxious for your life — what you shall eat;
>   For your body — what you shall wear.'
> Is not life more than food
> And the body than clothing? "
>
> (Matt. 6:25.)

This paragraph affords us a fascinating demonstration of the
truth of the point that we were discussing in Chapter VI with
reference to the Hebrew psychology (Matt. 5:29 f.). It will be
recalled that we were arguing there that the Hebrew looked
upon man's person as a unit rather than as a dichotomy composed of body and soul after the fashion of the Greek philoso-
phers. Accordingly, in the present passage we find at v. 25 a
parallelism of structure which clearly equates "life" and
"body," on the one hand, and "food" and "clothing," on the
other. "Life" in the Aramaic which our Lord was speaking is
often indeed used to express the reflexive pronoun " — self." [5]
Accordingly, the "body," as an essential part of the person, is
to be identified with one's "life" or "self" and shares in that
life's eternal character, whereas "food" and "clothing" are
evanescent or temporal adjuncts.

> " Look at the birds of the heavens
>   Which neither sow nor reap nor store:
>   Your Heavenly Father nourishes them —
>   Are you not more important than they?
>   In any case, which of you (by anxiety) can add to his
>   stature a cubit?
> Again, why worry about clothing?
> Consider the wild country lilies — how they grow!
>   They neither labor nor spin!
>   But I tell you, ' Solomon with all his splendor
>   Was not garbed like one of them! '
>   But if God so clothes a wild country reed —

> One that exists today
> And tomorrow is cast into an oven —
> Will he not much more you, O ' little-faith ' ones?
> Then, be not anxious, saying,
>   ' What are we to eat?
>   What are we to drink?
>   What are we to wear? '
> For it is for all these that the rest of men seek:
> For your Heavenly Father is aware that you need all these."
>
>   (Matt. 6:26–32.)

The teaching of these verses with the two examples of the " birds of the heavens " and the " wild country lilies " is so clear as to scarcely require comment. That Jesus followed the example of the prophets in believing that his Heavenly Father was not only Creator but also the Providential Governor of his universe goes without saying.[6] The poetic structure of this section appears clear in the English as in the Aramaic lying behind our Greek text. Numerous examples of parallelism, alliteration, and word play are found here by those acquainted with the Aramaic.[7]

> " But as for you, seek first the Kingdom of God and his right-
>   eousness,
> And all these will be added for you.
>
> Then be not anxious for the morrow,
> For the morrow will be anxious on its own:
> Sufficient for a day is its own evil! "
>
>   (Matt. 6:33 f.)

It should be obvious that our Lord in this passage is not suggesting that his disciples should practice asceticism. On the contrary, his point is that the Heavenly Father is interested in and understands the needs of men at every level of human existence. As was remarked in Chapter XI, Jesus taught his disciples that for this very reason they might pray for anything affecting their lives in any respect.

Jesus' teaching is rather that man should set before himself, as the goal for his life, the acceptance of the Lordship of God and the doing of God's righteous will, and that he should seek wholeheartedly that these be accomplished in his life. It is to this end that Jesus suggests the need of that spiritual insight which shall discern where the values of life really lie. He does not teach, therefore, that the evanescent things of life — man's ambitions, his family needs, his social and economic pursuits, and the like — are to be ignored or renounced. Rather, they are to be accepted but under the aegis of an overarching and all-embracing purpose and goal. In the light of that purpose and that goal, such things fall into perspective and find their proper place in man's interests and endeavors. The disciple of Jesus who sets before him the Lordship of God over his life will use all his attainments, his resources of whatever sort, his opportunities, his free time, to advance the will of God and to fulfill God's purpose for his life. It is this accepting of God's Lordship over one's life that Jesus had in mind when he said, " Whoever does not receive the Kingdom of God like a child shall not enter it " (Mark 10:15).

Verse 34 presents us with an anomaly. It finds no place in the Lucan text and appears to have been an addition of Matthew from his special source. The latter part of the verse almost appears to be flippant, and the suggestion has been made that it has no part in Jesus' teaching! [8] If the words are from Jesus' lips, possibly he was repeating a current, rather pessimistic proverb in an ironical vein simply to clinch his argument and the passage may be taken as an argument *ad hominem*.

D. HOW DOES THE CHRISTIAN BECOME THAT WAY?

CHAPTER XIII

Man's Lack of Kingdom Righteousness

Do not practice " sitting in judgment " lest you come in for judg-
ment!
For, by the sentence you render in judging, your judgment will
be made,
And with the standard you adopt in measuring, your measure
will be taken.
Why, then, glance at the splinter in your brother's eye,
While not recognizing the beam in your own?
Or, how can you say to your brother,
" Let me remove the splinter from your eye,"
While, look! the beam is in yours?
" Approval seeker," first remove the beam from your eye,
Then you will see clearly to remove the splinter from your brother's!

Give not a ring to dogs,
Cast not your pearls before swine,
Lest they trample them with their feet
And, turning, maul you.

(Matt. 7:1–6.)

As we have more than once observed during our study of
Matt., ch. 5, our Lord's teaching in the Sermon on the Mount
as elsewhere is of a character to justify the epithet of " an
absolute ethic " applied to it. As John Knox has remarked:
" Jesus was not trying to be practical, but to be true. He was
not seeking to state what man can do, but what God asks." [1]
It is obvious, too, that in the realm of religion Jesus taught that
God's demand was of the most exacting nature. As we have

seen, no less than utter sincerity and utter consecration would satisfy the righteous demand of God upon man.

In consequence, as his disciples heard such teaching, the question must have arisen again and again in their minds: " But is anyone this good? Can anyone be so perfect as this? If God's demand upon man is so utterly unattainable, is not man's condition quite hopeless in His sight? " Such questions were the more certain to arise in the minds of Jesus' disciples in view, on the one hand, of the note of authority which was to be discerned in such teaching (Matt. 7:28 f.), and, on the other, because the best religious teachers of the day (the scribes of the Pharisees) had by all accounts been teaching " a relative righteousness " only. Recognizing the utter impossibility of fulfilling the strict letter of the law's demands, the Pharisaic rabbis spent a good part of their professional careers in applying the law to practical life situations in a way to make it merely relatively workable.[2] The term " righteousness " carried with it for the Pharisee " no suggestion of sinless perfection " on man's part, for " God was too good, too reasonable, to demand a perfection of which he had created man incapable." [3]

In conscious opposition to the idea that God could be satisfied by anything other than absolute obedience on man's part, Jesus like Paul spoke as though he took the words of Ps. 14:1 ff. quite literally: " There is none that does good. . . . They have all gone astray, they are all alike corrupt; there is none that does good, no, not one." It would seem, indeed, that the fifth and sixth chapters of Matthew have the same motivation as the first three chapters of Romans, viz., to show that all men whether Jews or Gentiles without exception are sinners in the eyes of God.

It is, of course, impossible that any true revelation from God should state or imply that his demand in the realm of ethics and religion is less than absolute perfection. But it is equally impossible that man should measure up wholly to that perfect demand of God upon him. Every legalistic system, such as ancient Pharisaism and modern Islam, therefore, is faced with the dilemma of either writing the demands of God in a lower key or else of inflating man's ego to the point of imagining that he can really fulfill the impossible righteous demands of a Holy God, or both together.

One may well imagine, therefore, that Jesus' disciples, indoctrinated as they had been by the Pharisees who were largely in control of the synagogue and its teaching wherever it was found throughout Judaism, must have found our Lord's teaching incredible. The questions we have suggested above must have arisen in their minds again and again as he went on preaching the contents of Matt., chs. 5 and 6, and it is quite possible that one or another "exploded" with such questions as he finished what he had to say on the subject of utter consecration to the will of God. Whether such questions were actually asked or not, Jesus cannot but have realized that the minds and hearts of his hearers were in a turmoil. In consequence, in the passage before us we have the answer to these questions, spoken or unuttered.

For the thesis before us in the present passage is this: no mere man has ever measured up to the absolute standard set by God in the realms of ethics and religion. All men equally "live in glass houses and therefore dare not throw stones." All men "are in the same boat," and that boat is full of holes. In other words, there is but one category for men, and that is the category "sinners."

Certainly it is so that we are to understand Jesus' teaching in this passage beginning,

> " Do not practice ' sitting in judgment ' lest you come in for judgment!
>> For, by the sentence you render in judging, your judgment will be made,
>> And with the standard you adopt in measuring, your measure will be taken."
>
> (Matt. 7:1 f.)

It would be perfectly inane and quite out of the context, both of our Lord's present teaching and of the contemporary Judaism, to suppose that Jesus meant that his disciples were to refrain from making the small necessary judgments with regard to their friends' and contemporaries' abilities and shortcomings which are common to all social intercourse.

✗   The theme of the Sermon on the Mount as a whole is that of sin and its remedy. In consequence, if the present passage is to be understood as in context and apropos of the rest that our Lord has been teaching, then the " sitting in judgment " to which reference is made has to do with the pronouncement that this or that contemporary is " a sinner." Moreover, we know from the New Testament itself as well as from contemporary Jewish literature that the Pharisees were accustomed to divide all men into two categories of " righteous " and " sinners." It was with reference to this situation that Jesus replied to his scribal critics: " The healthy have no need of a physician but those who are ill. I did not come to call ' the righteous ' but ' sinners.' " (Mark 2:17.) The so-called *'amme ha-'aretz* (i.e., the people of the land) were generally termed by the Pharisees " unlearned and ignorant men " (Acts 4:13). There is a famous saying of the liberal Hillel with regard to such persons in the Mishnah to the effect that " an ignorant man (*'am ha-'aretz*) cannot be saintly " (M. Aboth 2:6).

It is possible, of course, to quote passages from the Jewish literature and from the New Testament itself in favor of a certain leniency in judgment on the part of particularly those who belonged to the school of Hillel. Hillel himself is said to have remarked, " Judge not thy fellow until thou art come to his place " (M. Aboth 2:5). The same book in the Mishnah contains a quotation said to come from Joshua ben Perahyah (120 B.C.): " When thou judgest any man, incline the balance in his favor " (1:6). Rabban Gamaliel the Elder, the teacher of the apostle Paul and the soft-spoken exponent of expediency in Acts 5:34-42, is a good example of worthy Pharisaism which abhorred harsh judgment meted out toward one's fellow men.

Nonetheless, there is far too much evidence both within the Gospels and current Jewish literature to suggest that it was the

Pharisees who considered themselves to be " righteous and scorned the rest of men " (Luke 18:9). It was undoubtedly such Pharisaism that divided all men into the two categories " righteous " and " sinners." And it was against such that Jesus uttered the parable of the Pharisee and the publican (Luke 18:10–14). It was such that blamed Jesus for being a friend of " publicans and sinners " (Luke 5:30). And it was against such that much of his invective was directed because of their legalistic standard of what constituted " righteousness " (Mark 2:13 ff.; see Matt. 5:20). There is a famous passage at M. Sanhedrin 10:1 which remarks that " all Israelites have a share in the world to come " because all are considered " righteous " in the sight of God. The same passage, however, immediately qualifies the statement with the remark that anyone who declares that " there is no resurrection of the dead " (a definitely Pharisaic doctrine), and any " Epicurean " (an expression intended to include all Gentiles and non-Pharisaic Jews) are to be excluded from the number of the saved!

Our Lord's teaching, on the contrary, allowed for no such dividing of men into the two categories of " righteous " and " sinners." His teaching that religion and ethics have to do, not with a series of particular commands to be observed as such, but rather with the attitude of the spirit, the motivation of the heart, clearly placed all men in the one category of " sinners." Surely then, it is of God's judgment that he speaks when he remarks, " For, by the sentence you render in judging, your judgment will be made, and with the standard you adopt in measuring, your measure will be taken." Strack-Billerbeck suggest that the passive construction as here was usually used by our Lord (in Matthew's Gospel at any rate) when an act of God was under consideration.[4] If this suggestion is correct, then Jesus would appear here to be saying that when the Pharisee condemns his brother as " a sinner," God is certain to do the same of him. And the following verses referring to the " splinter " and the " beam " obviously bear out the same thesis.

> " Why, then, glance at the splinter in your brother's eye,
>   While not recognizing the beam in your own?
>   Or, how can you say to your brother,
>   ' Let me remove the splinter from your eye,'
>   While, look! the beam is in yours?
>   ' Approval seeker,' first remove the beam from your eye,
>   Then you will see clearly to remove the splinter from your
>   brother's! "
>
> (Matt. 7:3–5.)

The point our Lord is making is that every man has in his own eye either the splinter or the beam. He has no right therefore to call his brother " sinner " and to consider himself " righteous." Strack-Billerbeck quote from the Talmud tractate Arakhin (16[b] Bar) a saying of Rabbi Tarfon (whose date was approximately A.D. 100) as follows: " I should be surprised if in this generation it were given to anyone to undertake to reprimand another. For if one should say to another, ' Take the splinter out of your eye,' the latter might very well answer, ' Take the beam out of your own eye.' " [5] It is quite possible, therefore, that the reference to " splinter " and " beam " as being in the eyes of one and another may have been a common contemporary metaphor for the presence of sin in men's lives. In any case, however, the use made of this metaphor is distinctly Jesus' own at this point.

If the teaching of Jesus against this Pharisaic self-righteousness is thought harsh, let it be recalled that he was dealing with a type of individual who in the name of religion was actually destroying the very thing for which he pretended to stand. There were certainly many good and sincere men among the Pharisees as there have always been and always will be among all religious groups anywhere in the world. The attitude of self-criticism which was found among them is one of the very best proofs of this fact. There is, for example, a saying that is to be credited to the rabbis not long after Jesus' day to the effect that there are seven kinds of Pharisees, of which only one is good. The seven categories are:

" The ' shoulder Pharisee,' who packs his good works on his shoulder (to be seen of men); the ' wait a bit' Pharisee, who (when someone has business with him) says, Wait a little; I must do a good work. The ' reckoning ' Pharisee, who when he commits a fault and does a good work crosses off one with the other; the ' economizing ' Pharisee, who asks, What economy can I practice to spare a little to do a good work? The ' show me my fault ' Pharisee, who says, Show me what sin I have committed, and I will do an equivalent good work (implying that he had no fault); the Pharisee of fear, like Job; the Pharisee of love, like Abraham."

Of these seven, the Jerusalem Talmud says, only the last is acceptable to God.[6]

When all that may be said in favor of Pharisaism as Jesus knew it has been said, however, it still remains that there must have been considerable religious exhibitionism among his contemporaries to give rise to the odium that we naturally have come to attach to the word " Pharisee." It is only that self-seeking, self-righteous variety against which Jesus' parables and invective were directed and of which it may be legitimately said: " ' Approval seeker,' first remove the beam from your eye, then you will see clearly to remove the splinter from your brother's! "

> " Give not a ring to dogs,
> Cast not your pearls before swine,
> Lest they trample you with their feet
> And, turning, maul you."
>
> (Matt. 7:6.)

This saying of our Lord (not found elsewhere) appears to break up the continuity of the argument of the chapter and has, therefore, often been considered as either a gloss introduced by Matthew into the teaching or else as a saying of Jesus wrongly inserted at this point.

However, it makes sense if considered as a pedagogical principle. Christianity is not and never has been a gnostic system with an esoteric teaching to be delivered only to those far advanced. There are no " mysteries " pertaining to our faith which may not be found openly stated on the clear pages of Scripture.

Nonetheless, it remains true that no pedagogue worthy of the name would consider teaching college subjects in the kindergarten class. No more is it wise to place the deepest spiritual truths or doctrines before those who have not had an adequate foundation laid for their reception. Our Lord himself is responsible for the maxim, "For whoever has to him it shall be given: and whoever has not even that which he has shall be taken from him" (Mark 4:25; see also Mark 4:11).

Moreover, on deeper thought, it would appear that the statement of such a pedagogical principle at this point in the argument is highly relevant. Jesus has just remarked that his disciples are not to "practice ' sitting in judgment'" on others. And yet the Christian teacher or evangelist must "sit in judgment" upon his auditors in the manner just indicated. Every Christian evangelist and teacher has done just this and must continue ever to do so. On this understanding of the text the "dogs" and "swine" will be those hearers who are unworthy of the deepest spiritual and moral truth which the Christian gospel has to present.

In our rendering of this verse we have accepted the suggestion of Matthew Black, that instead of the Greek reading "that which is holy," we should read "ring" as representing probably the original Aramaic spoken by Jesus at this point. In the Aramaic the difference between "that which is holy" (qudhsha) and "a ring" (q^{e}dhasha) is only the difference of the vowels, the consonants being the same in both cases. Black's suggestion at this point is the more acceptable as it serves to maintain the parallelism in the two parts of the saying, "ring" and "pearls" being very naturally opposed to one another.[7]

Chapter XIV

How the Righteousness Is Attained — God's Part

Ask — it will be given you;
Seek — you will find;
Knock — it will be opened to you.
　　For everyone asking receives,
　　Everyone seeking finds,
　　To everyone knocking there is opening.
Indeed, what man is there of you
　　Whose son shall ask him bread —
　　He will not dole out to him a stone, will he?
　　And if he shall request a fish —
　　He will not dole out to him a serpent, will he?
If, then, though evil you know to give good gifts to your children,
How much more will your Father in heaven give good things to
　　　　those asking him!
Then, everything that you wish men to do for you,
Do you also for them:
For this is the Law and the Prophets.

(Matt. 7:7–12.)

In no portion of the Sermon on the Mount is it clearer that we are dealing with the Aramaic poetry of our Lord than in the passage before us. The first six lines are obviously in parallel construction, two triplets in each of which but a single idea is intended to emerge. Moreover, there is in the first triplet a clear example of the Aramaic paratactic construction in which imperatives are grouped together — " ask," " seek," " knock." [1]

Similarly, in the paragraph beginning " Indeed, what man is there of you . . . ," there is a doublet in parallel construction or a triplet if the clause at Luke 11:12 (" Or, if he shall ask an egg, will he give him a scorpion ") is original. Also in the first line of this paragraph — " what man is there of you " — two Aramaic idioms occur, viz., the *casus pendens* [2] (i.e., as here, a nominative case hanging in air, so to speak) and the superfluous use of the noun for " man." [3] The concluding pronouncement in v. 11 is also characteristic of Jesus' poetical style and rounds out the stanza in the Aramaic poem.

The fact that Luke 11:9–13 contains this stanza almost verbatim but in another context is itself good evidence for its constituting a poetical unit in the original Aramaic of our Lord. That Luke should have the stanza there in the context of the Lord's Prayer and of the parable of the friend who came at midnight is not surprising. For wherever the stanza belongs, it should be obvious that its subject is prayer.

> " Ask — it will be given you;
> Seek — you will find;
> Knock — it will be opened to you.
> For everyone asking receives,
> Everyone seeking finds,
> To everyone knocking there is opening."
> (Matt. 7:7 f.)

Probably, however, no saying or poem of our Lord has been so taken out of context and misused as the passage before us. It is often supposed to have reference to prayer for the most mundane matters. One often hears the remark made that if one has lost a ring or a watch or a pen, this verse gives one to understand that he should pray to discover the same. The recovery then of the precious object in the haystack is supposed to be covered by the terms of Jesus' teaching on prayer at this point.

One would not wish to appear to rebuke such a naïve view of prayer. We have already seen that the petition in the Lord's Prayer — " Give us our bread day by day " — may well be understood as having reference to all of man's needs of whatever sort — material, intellectual, moral, even spiritual. Certainly our Lord, and the Christian faith as expressed in the writings of the

New Testament scriptures generally, never compartmentalized life. And both the Old and New Testaments are clear on the point that God is interested in every part of man's experience.

The problem before us at the moment, however, is not whether God is interested in all of our lives and experiences but whether in the stanza before us our Lord has a more specific reference in view. That to the mind of both Evangelists (Matthew and Luke) the more specific reference is present, rather than the general one, appears from at least two considerations.

First, Luke concludes the stanza as follows:

> "If, then, you though evil know to give good gifts to your children,
> How much more will the Father give the Holy Spirit from heaven to those who ask him."
>
> (Luke 11:13.)

It is quite true that there is much more on the Holy Spirit in Luke-Acts than in the other two Synoptic Gospels, and it might be argued that Luke had substituted "the Holy Spirit" for Matthew's "good things" in the conclusion to this stanza. The textual evidence is of a quite diverse nature. All the variants, however, it would seem, can be explained as differing endeavors to harmonize Luke's text with Matthew's. It is quite likely, therefore, that Luke found "the Holy Spirit" in the tradition which lay before him at this point. And if so, it is the spiritual and moral gifts of God to his children rather than those of a material or lower type, which Jesus had in mind in uttering the stanza.

Again, Matthew, although he has retained the "good things" which apparently lay in the form of the tradition which reached him, in his own way has indicated what he believed to be the relevance of the saying to our Lord's argument as a whole. For he has inserted it at exactly the point at which it is needed if our understanding of the thesis of the Sermon on the Mount is correct. We have already seen that in the stanza immediately preceding (Matt. 7:1–6), our Lord has been remark-

ing upon the general sinfulness of mankind. And in the conclusion of the present stanza, the phrase ("though evil") de-
scriptive of man generally appears to be a reference back to the
point of man's general sinfulness which has already been established. In the present stanza, then, the prayer introduced by
"ask," "seek," "knock" obviously would appear to have reference to the attainment of the righteousness which man lacks
and which God demands of him.

Since the Reformation, Protestants, under the influence of
Luther, have so largely stressed the so-called Pauline doctrine
of "justification by grace through faith" as to give the impression that salvation by grace is a distinctive discovery of the
apostle Paul. No greater mistake, however, could be made regarding the over-all teaching of Scripture. The Christian conception of the Old Testament which makes the "law," in the
sense of a group of commandments or ordinances, the great
word in the Old Testament is in reality a Pharisaic heresy! Likewise the thought that the Yahweh of the Old Testament is a
God of "wrath" while the Father of our Lord Jesus Christ is
a God of "love" is a heresy introduced into Christian thought
by the anti-Judaic Gnostic Marcion! [4]

In point of fact, it needs to be said with great vigor that the
God of the Old Testament is as clearly a God of love as is the
"Father of our Lord Jesus Christ." Surely in proof of this statement one needs to be reminded only of the forgiving love of
God elaborated in the dramatic prophecy of Hosea and of the
Servant Songs of Deutero-Isaiah, with their theme of vicarious
suffering with a view to the salvation of mankind.[5] Indeed, the
theme of the Old Testament from Gen., ch. 3, onward is God's
preparation of his people that it may be worthy morally and
spiritually to enjoy that fellowship with him which was broken
by man's rebellion against his will. Similarly, Paul's thesis in
the third chapter of Galatians (to the effect that the Law was
given in preparation for the Gospel of salvation previously an-
nounced to Abraham and fulfilled in Christ) finds verification
over and over again in the thesis of the prophets and psalms to

the effect that God is a redeeming God.[6]

It should be clear, then, that our Lord in his teaching at this point with regard to the *modus operandi* whereby man secures the righteousness God demands is simply in line with the teaching of the prophetic scriptures throughout. Man cannot attain that righteousness himself — such is the teaching of the Bible on its every page. God must give it to him because only God has the power and the will to give it.

Strack-Billerbeck once again at this point (as at Matt. 7:7 above) remark that the passives " it will be given you, it will be opened to you " reflect the contemporary rabbinical endeavor to refer to the action of God without using his name.[7] That their interpretation is correct needs no verification. If such be required, however, it will be found in the conclusion of the stanza at v. 11. For Jesus there suggests that men " though evil " can be gracious — " how much more," then, God! This sounds very much like Paul's teaching at Rom. 5:8 f.: " But God shows his love for us in that while we were yet sinners Christ died for us. . . . Much more shall we be saved by him from the wrath of God." T. W. Manson's statement then may stand as a sufficient summary of the teaching of the passage: " The blessings of the new age are not the fruit of ' progress ' or ' evolution ': they are the result of an act of God in history, his response to human needs and longings." [8]

> " Indeed, what man is there of you
>> Whose son shall ask him bread —
>> He will not dole out to him a stone, will he?
>> And if he shall request a fish —
>> He will not dole out to him a serpent, will he?
> If, then, though evil you know to give good gifts to your
> children,
> How much more will your Father in heaven give good things
> to those asking him! "
>
>   (Matt. 7:9–11.)

Regarding this third triplet — it is such if Luke's tradition at ch. 11:12 is added to that of Matthew, as indicated above on

page 152 — that in which opposition is expressed between
" bread " and " stone," between " fish " and " serpent," and
between " egg " and " scorpion," several points may be made.
As T. W. Manson remarks, the only one of these antitheses
common to both Matthew and Luke is that between " fish "
and " serpent," the other two being found respectively in one or
other Gospel.[9] This fact, however, is not to be taken as undoubted demonstration that these two anthitheses are not au-
thentic. The suggestion, for example, that the antithesis
" bread " and " stone " is a reflection of the first temptation of
our Lord appears rather naïve. The factual basis in common human experience for this antithesis is just as good as that for
the other two, if not better! In the East where " bread " usually consists of a flat, pancakelike piece of unleavened or un-
raised dough, it is certainly as similar to a " stone " as a " fish "
is to a " serpent " or an " egg " to a " scorpion "!

Again, if all three antitheses occurred in our Lord's teaching
at this point, Matthew may very well have dropped out the
third because of its comparative similarity to the second, and
Luke has similarly omitted the first because it did not seem to
go well with the other two! It is always difficult in a case like
this to discover where the juggling occurred in the tradition —
as between the Evangelists themselves, their sources, or even in
the usage of our Lord. On the whole, the triplet form best
suits the stanza, as in that case we have three triplets occurring one after the other and leading up to a single conclusion.

> " Then, everything that you wish men to do for you,
>   Do you also for them:
>   For this is the Law and the Prophets."
>
> (Matt. 7:12.)

The so-called " Golden Rule " appears in Luke at 6:31, a far
more suitable place for its appearing in our Lord's teaching than
here. Such teaching was on the whole not new with Jesus, constituting, as T. W. Manson has called it, merely a " rule of
thumb " to be used under certain ethical situations.[10]

Chapter XV

How the Righteousness Is Attained — Man's Part

Enter by the narrow gate —
> For wide is the gate and spacious the way leading to destruction,
> And many are they going in by it.
> How narrow is the gate and constricted the way leading to life!
> Few are they who find it.

Beware of prophets of lies
> Who come to you in clothing of sheep
> But within are rapacious wolves!
> It is by their fruits that you shall recognize them!
> They do not gather grapes from thorns nor figs from thistles, do they?
> Thus every good tree yields choice fruit
> And the bad tree yields rotten fruit.
> A good tree cannot yield rotten fruit
> Nor can a bad tree yield choice fruit.

(Every tree failing to yield choice fruit is hewn down and flung to the fire.)
So, then, it is by their fruits that you shall recognize them!

It is not everyone addressing me, " Lord, Lord,"
Who shall enter the Kingdom of Heaven,
But it is he who does the will of my Father in heaven
Who shall enter the Kingdom of Heaven.
Many will say to me in that day, " Lord, Lord,
> Was it not in thy name that we preached,
> In thy name that we exorcised demons,
> In thy name that we did miracles? "

Then, I shall confess to them, " I have never known you.
> Get you gone from me,
> You doers of unrighteousness."

Everyone, then, who hears these my words and does them
I should compare to a wise man
Who has built his house upon a rock.
    And the rain fell, the torrents came, the winds blew,
    And they surged upon the house:
    And it did not crash,
    For it was established upon a rock.
Everyone, also, who hears these my words and does them not
Should be compared to a simpleton
Who has built his house upon sand.
    And the rain fell, the torrents came, the winds blew,
    And they surged upon that house:
    And it crashed,
    And great was its fall.

(Matt. 7:13–27.)

In attaining the righteous demand of God upon his life, man as well as God has a part to play. This is what in theological terminology is generally called "synergism," or working together. With a view to exhibiting Jesus' teaching at this point, it will be found convenient to begin with a short statement about the outline and paragraphing of this somewhat lengthy passage. It clearly divides itself into the four stanzas which will be found in the translation. Each of these stanzas contains a short exposition of a doublet involved in Jesus' teaching. By stanzas these doublets will be found to be the following — (1) The Two Ways: to Death and to Life (vs. 13 f.); (2) The Two Prophets (vs. 15–20); (3) The Two Disciples (vs. 21–23); and (4) The Two Houses (vs. 24–27). We shall look at each of these in turn.

    " Enter by the narrow gate —
        For wide is the gate and spacious the way leading to
            destruction,
        And many are they going in by it.
        How narrow is the gate and constricted the way leading
            to life!
        Few are they who find it."

(Matt. 7:13 f.)

The doctrine of the " Two Ways " was by no means original with Jesus. It is found either explicitly or implicitly throughout the Old Testament scriptures and in the contemporary and later rabbinical literature. The earliest statement of it is to be found perhaps at Deut. 30:15, which reads: " See, I have set before you this day life and good, death and evil." Jeremiah has it in almost identical form: " Thus says the Lord: Behold, I set before you the way of life and the way of death " (Jer. 21:8). And it is, of course, by implication the teaching of Ps. 1 as a whole. " One of the earliest noncanonical references to the Two Ways " is found in I Enoch 92:19: " And walk in the paths of righteousness, and walk not in the paths of violence." [1] In II Enoch such teaching is referred to as that of the " two ways, the light and the darkness " (ch. 30:15). [2]

The doctrine also appears in the teachings of the Qumran sect. By implication it certainly appears in the Damascus Document at 2:1: " And I will disclose to you the ways of the wicked," as over against 9:42: " Then they spake each man with his neighbor to strengthen one another: ' Let our steps hold fast to the way of God.' " By implication the same doctrine is the theme also of the entire scroll known as " The War of the Sons of Light Against the Sons of Darkness," and one or other of the ways is referred to again and again in the Qumran texts, as for example the following: " I will choose the path He shows me, and be content with His judgments " (The Hymn of the Initiants); " (I will walk) the age-old way and the paths which Thou hast chosen " (Thanksgiving Hymn 4:4); " They that walk in the way Thou desirest have harkened unto me and rallied to Thy cause in the legion of the saints " (*ibid.*); and the like.

In M. Aboth 2:9 is to be found a famous discussion of the matter of the two ways. It will be sufficient here to quote the statement preceding the discussion on the two sides of the problem: " Go forth and see which is the good way to which a man should cleave " and " Go forth and see which is the evil way which a man should shun."

Jesus, then, uses this common teaching of both the Old Testament and contemporary Judaism with a view to challenging his contemporaries to follow in the constricted way of the new prophetic movement which he is inaugurating. We are not to conclude, as is sometimes done from the "many" and "few" which he employs, that in the end only a small group are to be saved through the preaching of the gospel! Clearly, he is describing the situation in his own day and the fact that the new "remnant" of which he is the leader is as yet constituted of a very small group of disciples. Also, though in a very general sense the terms "destruction" and "life" are eschatological ones, there is no evidence either here or elsewhere that Jesus was an apocalyptist holding that the resolution of the eternal issues pertaining to man's salvation must await the future. Jesus refused to answer the question of his disciples: "Are they few that are saved?" (Luke 13:23). Instead of a forthright answer, our Lord characteristically replied with the parable of the householder (Luke 13:22–30), whose moral is clearly: Your concern should be, not with a theoretical problem of the number of the saved, but rather that you are yourself one of the number whether few or many!

> " Beware of prophets of lies
>> Who come to you in clothing of sheep
>> But within are rapacious wolves!
>> It is by their fruits that you shall recognize them!
>> They do not gather grapes from thorns nor figs from
>>> thistles, do they?
>> Thus every good tree yields choice fruit
>> And the bad tree yields rotten fruit.
>> A good tree cannot yield rotten fruit
>> Nor can a bad tree yield choice fruit.
> (Every tree failing to yield choice fruit is hewn down and flung
>> to the fire.)
> So, then, it is by their fruits that you shall recognize them! "
>>   (Matt. 7:15–20.)

The comparison of the two prophets — the false and the true — which occurs in this stanza is one familiar to all readers of the Old Testament scriptures. A good description of the false prophet occurs in Deut. 13:1-3, and the familiar incidents wherein Michaiah ben Imlah and Elijah were forced willy-nilly into controversy with this sort of prophet are but two examples of what was evidently a common experience of the true prophet in ancient Israel (I Kings 18:20-46; 22:1-28). As these and the like incident serve to indicate, the "false prophet" in ancient Israel and Judah was apparently the typical "yes man" of the reigning monarch, a nationalist and therefore a political figure not to be despised.[3]

The Curatonian Syriac at this point has for "prophets of lies" the two words *nebhie deshuqre*, to be translated literally "prophets of lies." *Shuqre* ("lies") is the Aramaic noun of the same stem as the adjective that we translated "approval seekers" at Matt. 6:2 ff.[4] By these hypocrites or lying prophets, therefore it would appear that Jesus has reference to the political opportunists of his own day — the equivalents of those in ancient Israel and Judah. And we know from the sources available to us both within and outside the New Testament that these included all the religious leaders in the contemporary Judaism — those of the Pharisaic, Sadducaic, and Zealot groups. If we may believe that the "eschatological discourse," found in Mark, ch. 13, and in the parallel passages in the other Gospels, is from the lips of Jesus (as I personally believe to have been the case), then both there and here our Lord is warning his disciples against such political opportunism as endeavors to capitalize on its religious affiliations. It was, of course, out of such political opportunism that the "false messiahs" referred to in the "eschatological address" (Mark 13:22) took their rise. It was also against the temptation to adopt such a political affiliation that Jesus had to battle in his own temptations (Matt. 4:1 ff.).[5] In the book of The Revelation the "false prophet" par excellence was the Imperial Cultus (see chs. 16:13; 19:20; 20:10).

Our Lord's reference to such political opportunists as wolves in sheep's clothing appears to find no parallel in the contemporary Jewish literature.[6] Moreover, his statement in v. 16 and again in v. 20 to the effect that " it is by their fruits that you shall recognize them" appears to have as its nearest Biblical parallel Prov. 20:11 — " Even a child makes himself known by his acts " — nor is there any parallel to such teaching in the rabbinical literature. The five lines in parallel construction that follow, with the references to thorns, thistles, trees and their fruit, lay the stress upon the central nature of man's person — his inner self and its motivation.[7] I have placed the line reading " Every tree failing to yield choice fruit is hewn down and flung to the fire " in parenthesis, both because it is not in the parallel passage at Luke 6:43-45 and therefore was probably not in " Q " and also because it appears to reflect the apocalyptic teaching of John the Baptist as found in Matt. 3:10 and parallel passages.

> " It is not everyone addressing me, ' Lord, Lord,'
>   Who shall enter the Kingdom of Heaven,
>   But it is he who does the will of my Father in heaven
>   Who shall enter the Kingdom of Heaven.
>   Many will say to me in that day, ' Lord, Lord,
>   Was it not in thy name that we preached,
>   In thy name that we exorcised demons,
>   In thy name that we did miracles? '
>   Then, I shall confess to them, ' I have never known you.
>   Get you gone from me,
>   You doers of unrighteousness.' "
>
>   (Matt. 7:21-23.)

In this stanza relating to the two types of disciples, the point is abundantly clear that Jesus wants neither lip service (" It is not everyone addressing me, ' Lord, Lord,' ") nor a type of religious exhibitionism which lays stress upon pious labors (" we preached," " we exorcised demons," and " we did miracles "). Such disciples, on our Lord's own testimony, are nothing but " doers of unrighteousness," that is, disciples whose righteousness does not measure up to the high demand God makes upon human life.

If our Lord desires, then, neither lip service nor good deeds as such, the question not unnaturally arises, What is it that does fulfill God's righteous demand upon man? Jesus himself says that it is the doing of " the will of my Father in heaven." But in itself this statement is not clear. For answer one must return to the remarks we have been making with regard to Jesus' teaching in the Sermon as a whole. And from this larger context it becomes clear that what Jesus desires of man is neither words nor deeds as such, but rather a pure heart and a right attitude within. It is such motivation — the about-face of the personality, the securing of right direction along the way of life, the resolute purpose to walk in the way of God's will for one's life — that fulfills the will of the Father in heaven for man.

It is easy to infer that the entering of the Kingdom of Heaven which is had in mind here is of an eschatological sort, though this is by no means necessarily the case. As we have already seen, at Mark 10:15, to " enter the Kingdom of Heaven " may have reference to the joining of the eternal fellowship on earth. In either case, of course, it is with the eternal issues of life that our Lord is dealing at this point. Perhaps, however, the most certain eschatological note in the stanza as a whole is the phrase " in that day," which, like the similar reference to the " day " and " hour " at Mark 13:32, probably refers to " the day of the Lord " or " the day of judgment " in which all Jews have believed from the time of Amos onward, at least.[8]

The argument which the disciples are said to put forward to their Lord " in that day " differs markedly in the two versions of Matthew here and at Luke 13:26 f. For in Matthew their claim is that they have fulfilled the sort of program that Jesus laid down for his disciples on their first missionary journey at ch. 10:7–8. In the Lucan version, on the other hand, the argument runs: " We ate and drank in your presence, and you taught in our streets." [9] Here the argument obviously proceeds, not on the basis of service, but rather of fellowship. The conclu-

sion seems unavoidable that Matthew and Luke are quoting
here two opposite sources in the tradition that lay before
them.[10]

> " Everyone, then, who hears these my words and does them
> I should compare to a wise man
> Who has built his house upon a rock.
>> And the rain fell, the torrents came, the winds blew,
>> And they surged upon the house:
>> And it did not crash,
>> For it was established upon a rock.
> Everyone, also, who hears these my words and does them
>   not
> Should be compared to a simpleton
> Who has built his house upon sand.
>> And the rain fell, the torrents came, the winds blew,
>> And they surged upon that house:
>> And it crashed,
>> And great was its fall."
>
>   (Matt. 7:24–27.)

The last stanza of our passage containing the double parable
of the houses built upon the firm and the insecure foundations
forms a fitting conclusion to the Sermon as a whole. It issues a
clarion call to Jesus' disciples to follow his teaching implicitly.
The life of such disciples only may be thought secure because
it is founded on sure foundation, that, namely, of our Lord's
teaching of the gospel message.

Strack-Billerbeck quote a parable from the mouth of Rabbi
Elisha ben Abuja of about A.D. 120, which runs along lines quite
similar to that of our Lord in this stanza.[11] The moral of the
parables in the two cases is alike in that in both the foundations
of the houses are indicated as the determining factor in the future course of the lives for which the houses stand. The two
parables differ, however, markedly in the teaching they contain
— the teaching of the rabbi suggesting, in harmony with the
Judaism of the day, that " good works and the observance of the
Torah " and the teaching of Jesus that the observing of the
terms of the gospel, will respectively lead to salvation.[12]

The Effectiveness of Jesus' Preaching

And so it came to pass —
When Jesus had finished these his words —
That the assembled crowds were amazed at the character of his in-
struction:
For as an authority he was teaching them,
And not as their rabbis and the Pharisees.

(Matt. 7:28–29.)

We come now, in the epilogue to the Sermon on the Mount,
to look at the Evangelist's witness to the effectiveness of Jesus'
teaching. The record of astonishment attending Jesus' teaching
and miraculous works is a common one in the various traditions
underlying the Gospel narratives. Mark records the fact, for example, that in the early days of Jesus' synagogue ministry at
Capernaum, after he had finished teaching, " they were astonished at his teaching, for he taught them as one who had authority, and not as the scribes" (Mark 1:22). Luke, too, remarks of those early days when he taught in the synagogues:
" All spoke well of him, and wondered at the gracious words
which proceeded out of his mouth" (Luke 4:22). Mark says
further that when Jesus taught in the synagogue " in his own
country" those who heard him " were astonished, saying,
' Where did this man get all this? What is the wisdom given
to him? What mighty works are wrought by his hands!'"
(Mark 6:2). John also reports that as a result of Jesus' teaching
" some of the people said, ' This is really the prophet.' Others

said, 'This is the Christ'" (John 7:40 f.).

The terminology employed in these passages is important. In one way or another in all of them the uniqueness of Jesus as teacher is clearly evident. The people discern the fact that he is not as their scribes and the Pharisees. They place him rather in the category of "prophet," "Messiah," or simply of "one who had authority." That is to say, there was about his teaching a distinctively creative or original quality unlike that of the scribes, who depended for their authority upon "tradition."

Both Mishnah and Talmud bear witness to the fact that the scribes and Pharisees leaned heavily upon tradition for the authority attaching to their teachings. The usual formula runs something like this: "Rabbi X says, on the authority of Rabbi Y, who again received his teaching from Rabbi Z." Indeed in the very "holy of holies" of the Mishnah, in the book entitled Pirke Aboth, which means "the sayings of the fathers," the endeavor is made to show that all the traditional teaching of the rabbis goes back in the first instance to Moses himself, who received the oral law as well as the written from God on Mount Sinai (1:1).

Little wonder that the Jewish people of Jesus' time, who had been accustomed to this sort of distant leaning upon tradition for the authority of their teachings on the part of the scribes, were deeply impressed by Jesus' words when he said, "You have heard that it has been said. . . . But I say to you." Here was a type of authoritative teaching which, if anything, went even beyond the prophets who could say only, "Thus says the Lord." Jesus said rather, "Thus say I." T. W. Manson, in endeavoring to trace out the difference between the authority of the scribes and even of the prophets on the one hand and of Jesus on the other, finds "the foundation of it in his unique spiritual experience." The experience in question says Manson, is that which takes place "at Jordan which initiates his public activity." Manson rightly, in our judgment, further analyzes as follows the difference which this experience makes for Jesus: "The prophetic commission is relative to a given historical situation; the filial relation is independent of place, time, or circumstances. The descent of the Holy Spirit, too, signifies something permanent. It is not that Jesus receives an inspired message, but that the spiritual source of all inspiration takes possession of him, so that when he speaks it is not that he repeats words given to him but that the Spirit of his Father speaks in him." [1]

From the expression here in v. 29 — "as an authority he was teaching them" — Strack-Billerbeck conclude, "Jesus taught not from himself as one who was merely a good thinker, rather as a prophet who spoke from the mouth of God." [2] Similarly, Rabbi Israel Abrahams some years ago suggested that behind the Evangelist's expression in these passages in which the term "authority" occurs is the Hebrew expression *mi pi ha Gaburrah* ("out of the mouth of Power"), a phrase in which the term *Gaburrah* or Power is a pious equivalent employed by the rabbis that they might not be required to pronounce the Hebrew name for God. [3] Both of these writers appear to mean the same thing, viz., that Jesus' authority for his teaching was the direct authority of the God who spoke in and through him. And this was even more than the authority of a prophet, it was rather that of the Incarnate Word himself.

It was thus that Jesus preached and taught in all the synagogues of Galilee "the gospel of the Kingdom" (Matt. 4:23). He became for his contemporaries, and has since been for all the world, that Herald prophesied by Isaiah (ch. 52:7), of whom the prophet said:

> "How beautiful upon the mountains are the feet of him
> Who brings the gospel,
> Who publishes peace,
> Who brings the gospel of good,
> Who publishes salvation,
> Who says to Zion, ' Your God has begun his reign.' "

As Herald of the new day, Jesus embodied in his own person the gospel of the Kingdom of God which he preached. [4]

Notes

Symbols employed
CAP — R. H. Charles, *Apocrypha and Pseudepigrapha of the Old Testament*, 2 vols. (1913).
KW — G. Kittel, *Theologisches Wörterbuch zum Neuen Testament*, Vols. I–VI (1933–   ).
MB — Matthew Black, *An Aramaic Approach to the Gospels and Acts*, 2d edition (1954).
MJ — G. F. Moore, *Judaism*, 3 vols. (1927–1930).
MMW — Major, Manson, and Wright, *The Mission and Message of Jesus* (1938).
MTS — T. W. Manson, *The Teaching of Jesus*, 2d edition (1935).
S-B — Strack and Billerbeck, *Kommentar zum N. T. aus Talmud und Midrash*, 4 vols. (1922–1928).

Introduction

1 Cf. the author's *The Intention of Jesus* (1943), p. 131, and Appendix B, pp. 231–236; also the argument of MTS for his use of Rabbinic Hebrew and the respect shown him by his enemies, pp. 46–50, as well as Matthew Black's acceptance of Manson's thesis in MB, p. 14.

2 MTS, p. 69.

3 *Die Gleichnisreden Jesu* (2d edition, 1899), Vol. I, pp. vii f.

4 J. Jeremias, *The Parables of Jesus* (1954), pp. 52–70; T. W. Manson, *The Sayings of Jesus* (1949), p. 35; C. H. Dodd, *The Parables of the Kingdom* (3d edition, 1936), pp. 1–13 ff.

5 Extreme form critics who adopt the "Messianic secret" theory of Wilhelm Wrede of course look with suspicion on every teaching that purports to have been given to his disciples by our Lord

" in secret " (Mark 4:10). R. Bultmann may be taken as the outstanding example of this type of critic. Cf. his *Theology of the
New Testament* (1951), Vol. I, pp. 26–32.

6 MTS, pp. 50–56; MB, pp. 258 ff., *et passim*.

7 J. Wellhausen, *Einleitung in die drei ersten Evangelien* (2d
edition, 1911); C. F. Burney, *The Poetry of Our Lord* (1925);
F. Schulthess, *Grammatik des Christlich-Palästinischen Ara-
mäisch* (1924), and *Lexicon Syropalaestinum* (1903).

8 MTS, pp. 50 ff.; C. F. Burney, *op. cit.*, pp. 15 ff.; Vincent Taylor,
The Formation of the Gospel Tradition (1933), pp. 88 ff.

9 So MB, p. 119.

10 For example, at Mark 10:21, 27, 39 f., 42–45, etc.

11 MTS, p. 56, note 1. The writer endeavored to have the poetical
structure of our Lord's teaching made plain in connection with
the publication both of *The Westminster Study Edition of The
Holy Bible* (1948) and the Revised Standard Version (1952) to
no avail!

12 B. S. Easton, *The Gospel Before the Gospels* (1928), p. 124.

13 When learning his first lessons in Greek, the writer noted that
the lexicon contained as a definition for the adjective *plesios*
the following: " close, close together, near together, compact,
dense." Rapid pronunciation of this definition exhibits a rhythm
like that for which American college yells are famous! One could
never forget the exact wording of such a definition.

Prologue

1 Incidentally, it seems to me that C. H. Dodd in his work entitled *Gospel and Law* (1951) has oversimplified the relation
between these two elements of the Christian faith when he
equates gospel with *kerygma* and Christian *Haggadah*, on the
one hand, and law with *didache* or *Torah* and *Halakhah*, on the
other (pp. 9 ff.). In point of fact, Torah and *didache* both mean
instruction and should be equated, in my judgment. Both gospel
(*Haggadah*) and ethics or law (*Halakhah*), then, are to be sub-
sumed under Torah or *didache*. When these equations are made,
it becomes intelligible that the Sermon on the Mount should be
called both " gospel " (Matt. 4:23) and " teaching " (chs. 5:2;
7:28).

2 MJ, Vol. III, p. 104, note 92.

3 The sanest account of the meaning of such terms as " Belial,
or Satan, or Mastema, or Azazel " — all of which stand in the

popular jargon of the apocalyptic and other literature contemporary with the beginning of the Christian movement for one and the same series of ideas — is to be found in H. H. Rowley's *The Relevance of Apocalyptic* (2d edition, 1947), pp. 155–163, particularly at p. 162, note 1. Cf. also the author's *The Drama of the Book of Revelation* (1955), pp. 64, 65, 81, 135.

4 A. M. Hunter, *The Work and Words of Jesus* (1950), Appendixes, pp. 131–192; Julian Price Love, *The Gospel and the Gospels* (1953), pp. 15–23.

5 Cf. the author's article in *The Journal of Bible and Religion* for July, 1947 (Vol. XV, 3, pp. 162–170), entitled " An Exposition of the Beatitudes."

Chapter I

1 The contents of Chapters I and II represent a rewriting of the author's article in *The Journal of Bible and Religion* for July, 1947, pp. 162–170, entitled " An Exposition of the Beatitudes." The author herewith tenders his thanks to the editor for permission to use this material.

2 Thus Hauck writes in KW (1942), Vol. IV, p. 370: " The New Testament favors — as often similarly the LXX — a predicative *makarios* placed at the beginning of the sentence, following which comes the article with the name of the person to be blessed (cf. Matt. 5:3 ff.; Rev. 1:3; 14:13; etc.) and at times in a subordinate clause the reason for or description of the nature of the salvation to be achieved (*hoti* — Matt. 5:3 ff.; Luke 1:45; etc.)."

3 This point is made by Hauck in the above-mentioned article when he remarks that the Greek words from the stem *makar* find their peculiar significance in the New Testament in this, that " in the majority of cases they allude to the peculiarly religious joy which accrues to a man through his partaking in the salvation offered by the Kingdom of God " (pp. 369 f.).

4 Cf. his *Jewish Theology* (1918), p. 487.

5 W. C. Allen, *Commentary on Matthew* (3d edition, 1912), *ad loc.*

6 *Ibid., ad loc.*

7 W. O. E. Oesterley, *The Psalms* (1939), Vol. I, pp. 222, 225.

8 In keeping with what is said at this point in the text, it is instructive to note that E. L. Sukenik in the volume entitled *The Dead Sea Scrolls of the Hebrew University* (1955) remarks: " He [the scribe of ' The War of the Sons of Light with the

Sons of Darkness'] distinguished clearly between every letter of the alphabet, except ' yodh ' and ' waw,' which are throughout interchangeable " (p. 35).

⁹ Cf. his *Commentary on Isaiah* (Cambridge Bible), Vol. II, pp. 240, 242.

¹⁰ I am rejecting at this point, of course, the well-known theory of the school of " consistent eschatology " to the effect that the Sermon on the Mount as a whole was intended for a short period during which Jesus' immediate disciples should await the coming of the Kingdom of God in the final meaning of the term at the end of the age.

Chapter II

¹ Edwyn Hoskyns and Noel Davey, *The Riddle of the New Testament* (1931), p. 38.

² MJ, Vol. II, pp. 194 f.

³ There appears to be one exception to this at Neh. 7:2, where, however, the context makes it clear that the meaning of the term is " faithful," or perhaps better " man of truth " (cf. " men of truth " at Ex. 18:21). Proverbs 14:25 also uses the term as an adjective modifying " witness " — an ideal abstraction.

⁴ The word substituted for *'emeth* is *ken*; while some of the substituted words or phrases are *bar lebab* (" pure at heart "), *tahor* or *taher* (" pure," " clean "), *zak* (" pure," " clean "), *yashar* (" straight," " even "), *'emum* (" faithful ").

⁵ Briggs, *The Psalms* (1906), p. 231.

⁶ Oesterley has made the interesting suggestion that " the restoration of Jacob " referred to in v. 1 (*sᵉbuth ya 'aqob*) is the technical phrase used by the prophets generally for " the bringing back of the time of primeval happiness, the ' Golden Age,' " as as this was " adopted by the prophets, who interpreted it as in reference to the ' Messianic Age ' " (cf. Amos 9:14; Jer. 33:14–16). The psalm is thus an " eschatological psalm," as both Duhm and Buttenwieser also agree. Cf. Oesterley, *The Psalms* (1939), Vol. II, pp. 382 f.; Duhm, *Psalmen* (1922), p. 217; Briggs, *op. cit.*

⁷ The fact should not escape our observation that, if this conclusion is accepted, then the techniques of both literary and form criticism failed to solve this problem. It should be obvious, therefore, that however excellent they may be (and are, in my judgment), they need constantly to be checked with the equally adequate methods employed by the sciences of linguistics and of Biblical theology.

8 M. Buttenwieser, *The Psalms* (1938), p. 273; W. O. E. Oesterley, *The Psalms* (1939), Vol. II, p. 386.
9 This fact, be it noted, is another — and perhaps one should say,
final — demonstration that the Beatitudes of the second stanza
are from Jesus and not the creation of the church, for there can
be no doubt that the eschatology of the church was of the
apocalyptic type.

Chapter III

1 On the poetic structure of these paragraphs and the parallels
in Luke 6:22 f.; 14:34 f., cf. MB, pp. 123 ff., 258 ff., 274 ff., and
C. F. Burney, *Poetry*, pp. 130 f.
2 *The Intention of Jesus*, pp. 148 f.; C. H. Dodd, *According to the
Scriptures* (1953), pp. 118–121.
3 W. M. Albright, *From the Stone Age to Christianity* (1940),
pp. 254 f.
4 Ignatius, Epistle to the Romans, IV, edited by E. J. Goodspeed,
The Apostolic Fathers (1950), p. 222.
5 MTS, pp. 203–204.
6 MB, pp. 98, 259, 275 f.
7 Cf. for the saying about salt, S-B, Vol. I, p. 235.
8 MB, pp. 124 f.
9 C. K. Barrett, *The Gospel According to St. John* (1955), pp.
131–132; cf. C. H. Dodd, *The Interpretation of the Fourth Gospel* (1953), pp. 202–204.
10 MTS, p. 92; S-B, Vol. I, p. 392.

Chapter IV

1 That Jesus Christ in his historic activity was the culmination
of the redemptive-revelational process was Oscar Cullmann's
theme in Part II of his *Christ and Time* (1950), particularly
Chapter 1 of the part, pp. 121 ff.; it had previously been my own
thesis in *The Intention of Jesus* (1943); cf. especially Chapter
II, pp. 43 ff.; cf. also *Prophetic Realism and the Gospel* (1955),
pp. 106 *et passim*.
2 MJ, Vol. I, Part II, Chapter II, " The Scriptures," pp. 235 ff.
3 The problem of " fasting " at Mark 2:18–22 gave our Lord the
occasion to reply, in terms of the parable of the bridegroom and
his guests and the parable of the new wine and the old wineskins, on his attitude toward the old revelation and its sacra-

mental expression. He will not perpetuate the old forms, but also he will not destroy them — " the wine will burst the skins "; and he is not concerned alone that then " the wine is lost," but also that " so are the skins." The old is sacred in his eyes as well as the new!

4 Cf. Delling in KW, Vol. VI, pp. 292 f.

5 MTS, pp. 36, 304², and MMW, *ad loc.*

6 Hans Windisch, *The Meaning of the Sermon on the Mount* (1951), pp. 130 ff.

7 In v. 20 occurs an exceptional construction — *perisseuse* followed by *pleion.* The usual Greek construction is for this verb to be followed by *para* or *hyper* with the accusative. The Palestinian Syriac reads " *ethyathar . . . saghi men,*" the proper Aramaic for " be increased more than." The Greek looks like a literal translation of the Aramaic!

Chapter V

1 The Hebrew (*hen, chesed*) and Greek (*eleos, charis*) words for " mercy " and " grace " are practically interchangeable; so Barth's statement applies in the present context.

2 MB, p. 235.

3 Both words (*reqa* and *more*) are terms of contempt. The former is certainly Aramaic and the latter may be so. Cf. T. W. Manson, MMW, *in loco.*

4 Damascus Document, XVII, in Millar Burrows, *The Dead Sea Scrolls* (1955), pp. 362 f.

5 The Manual of Discipline, III, in *ibid.,* pp. 378 f.

6 MB, p. 197.

7 T. W. Manson, MMW, p. 414.

Chapter VI

1 Cf. pp. 67 f. and MB, p. 235.

2 It should be remembered, as Millar Burrows has pointed out, that for the Hebrews the family was the basic social unit. Hebrew conceptions of the relations between the sexes were motivated by the wish to perpetuate the family. Marriage was more a concern of the family than of the individual. Thus, the implication of the law (though not always so understood) is behind Jesus' statement in the verses here under consideration, i.e., " to the Christian man every woman is a sister, respected as a person, who

cannot be treated or even thought of as a mere instrument of his advantage or pleasure." (Cf. Millar Burrows, *An Outline of Biblical Theology* (1946), pp. 294 f.)

3 T. W. Manson, MMW, p. 315.

4 Vincent Taylor, *Commentary on Mark*, p. 408.

5 H. Wheeler Robinson, who is a pioneer in the study of Hebrew psychology, remarks that there is no trichotomy in Hebrew psychology, no triple division of human personality into "body, soul, and spirit." He says further: "An exhaustive description of human personality was given by saying ' body and soul' (*basar*, flesh, and *nephesh*, soul, as in Isa. 10:18). But even the phrase ' body and soul' would mislead a modern reader, influenced far more than he realizes by Greek and modern psychology. There is not even a dichotomy in the strict sense of the word. The Hebrew idea of personality is an animated body, not an incarnated soul." Cf. H. Wheeler Robinson, "The Hebrew Psychology," in *The People and the Book*, edited by A. S. Peake (1925), pp. 362 f.

6 MJ, Vol. II, p. 380: "After they thus appeared just as they had been, God would heal them of all their infirmities."

7 The references are: Matt. 5:22, 29, 30; 10:28 (Luke 12:5); 18:9 (Mark 9:43, 45, 47); 23:15, 33.

8 S-B, Vol. II, pp. 1029 ff.; I. Abrahams, *Pharisaism and the Gospels*, Vol. II, pp. 41–49; and I Enoch 27:2; 4 Ezra 7:36; M. Aboth 1:5; 5:19; Tos. Sanhedrin 13:3.

9 T. W. Manson, MMW, p. 127.

10 These include Codex Bezae, 64, and the Old Latin MSS. a, b, k. Hort indicated his doubt about the sentence by placing it in brackets.

Chapter VII

1 Cf. H. Wheeler Robinson, *Redemption and Revelation* (1942), p. 299; and I Kings 3:26; Ps. 7:9; 16:7; 26:2; 73:21; 139:13; Jer. 31:20; Mark 3:5; Luke 16:15; Rom. 2:29; Phil. 2:1; Col. 3:12; Rev. 2:23.

2 See the distinction between "vows" and "oaths" given by Canon Danby in the *Mishnah* (1933), p. 264, note 1.

3 Cf. the discussion on this subject in S-B, *in loco*, and by T. W. Manson, MMW, pp. 450 f.

4 Cf. M. Nedarim 1:3. For a discussion of this topic and much more material to the same effect from the Jewish literature of the period, one may refer to S-B, Vol. I, pp. 3–28 ff.

5 There are rabbinic parallels to this saying of Jesus, as for instance

that of Rabbi Huna who flourished about A.D. 350, and who said,
" The yes (*hen*) of the righteous is a yes (*hen*), and their no
(*lo*) is a no (*lo*)." S-B, *in loco.*

Chapter VIII

[1] Cf. also Ex. 21:23–25; Deut. 19:21.

[2] *Op. cit.,* Vol. I, pp. 337 ff. Two quotations from the Talmud
may be taken as illustrations of this point: In Hagigah 1:11b:
" For it is taught, Rabbi said ' Life for life ' means monetary
compensation. You say it means monetary compensation; but
perhaps it means actual life? " And in Sanhedrin 9:79a: Rabbi
Eleazer observed: " The verse refers to attempted murder, because it is written, ' And if any mischief follow, then thou shalt
give life for life.' But how does Rabbi Simeon interpret ' thou
shalt give life for life '? . . . It refers to monetary compensation." Cf. also Kethuboth 3:32b, 33a.

[3] It is interesting to note that modern psychopathology finds in
such people some of the symptoms of the paranoid personality.
" Their favorite attitude seems to be, ' Nobody is going to push
me around.' They are often an extremely disturbing and antago-
nistic element of society. They may take legal steps to protect their
personal rights and to correct what they consider to be unfair
circumstances directed against them. They have been, as a result referred to as ' litigious personalities.' " English and Pear-
son, *Emotional Problems of Living* (1955), p. 495.

[4] C. F. Burney, *The Poetry of Our Lord,* p. 169; T. W. Manson,
MMW, *in loco.*

[5] MB, p. 273. On pages 137 and 138 Black considerably recon-
structs Luke's terminology and the order of the sayings and
thereby is able to produce in the Aramaic a better poetical form
including various types of parallelism, alliteration, assonance, and
word play.

[6] The evidence for the addition " yet other " before the word
" two " is: D, *lat, syr* [sin]*, Ireneus.*

Chapter IX

[1] The suggestion is that of S-B, Vol. I, p. 353. The same authors
suggest that the nearest to the total saying to be found in the
Old Testament is at II Sam. 19:6-7.

2 Cf. Deut. 20:13–18; Josh. 10:40; 11:14, 19; Ps. 137:9.

3 J. A. Bewer, *The Literature of the Old Testament* (1933), p. 186.

4 T. W. Manson in MMW, p. 453: "There was nothing in Lev. 19:18 to indicate to a Jew in the days of Jesus that he ought to love Pontius Pilate."

5 MJ, Vol. II, pp. 85 f. and note 5 on p. 85.

6 *Ibid.*, Vol. II, p. 142.

7 *Ibid.*, Vol. II, p. 150.

8 Cf. IV Esdras 13:34 and Ecclus. 47:11.

9 *The Mishnah*, p. 397.

10 The nearest thing to our Lord's teaching at this point is to be found in some of the extracanonical literature; see my discussion in *The Religion of Maturity*, pp. 188–189.

11 MB (pp. 137 f.) has a valuable discussion on the poetical structure of this passage in Luke. He suggests, however, some rearrangement of the verses which to my mind is unconvincing.

12 Cf. *Bible Key Words* (1951), pp. 25 f. Also, Alan Richardson, *A Theological Word Book of the Bible* (1950), pp. 131 f.

13 The following are the relevant passages for a further study of the various forms of the Golden Rule:

Shabbath 31a (Hillel): "What is hateful to you, do not to your neighbor: that is the whole Torah, while the rest is commentary thereof: go and learn it."

Letter of Aristeas (paragraph 207): Advice to a king: "As thou desirest that evils should not befall thee, but to partake of all that is good, thou should act in this spirit to thy subjects and to offenders."

Didache 1:2: "Love those that hate you and you will have no enemy."

Tobit 4:15: "What thou hatest, do to no man."

Test. of Issachar 5:2: "Love the Lord and your neighbor, and have compassion on the poor and feeble."

Cf. also Test. of Naphtali 1; Test. of Daniel 5:3; Philo in Eusebius "Preparation for the Gospel" viii: 7:6; and the "Western" text of Acts 15:29.

Chapter X

1 On the whole subject, cf. S-B, Vol. I, pp. 386 ff., and Schrenk in KW, art. *dikaiosune*, Vol. II, pp. 198 ff.

2 That the reading "righteousness" is undoubtedly right in v. 1,

which then constitutes a " title for the entire passage in vs. 2–
18," cf. S-B, Vol. I, p. 386.

3 MJ, Vol. I, p. 4; and Ezra 7:6, 11, 12; Neh. 8:1, 4.

4 CAP, Vol. I, pp. 197, 283.

5 MJ, Vol. II, pp. 171 f.

6 Cf. Theodor H. Gaster, *The Dead Sea Scriptures* (1956), p. 39.

7 *Ibid.*, p. 83.

8 The translation " approval seekers " is an almost exact rendering
of the Syriac *nosebh deaphe*. The same Syriac expression occurs
at Acts 10:34. For other suggestions, cf. MB, pp. 133 ff. and S-B,
Vol. I, p. 388.

9 The Syriac and Aramaic for this would be *baita selutha*, that is,
literally " house of prayer."

10 MB, pp. 133 ff.

Chapter XI

1 Lagrange, *Evangile selon Sant Luc* (1921), pp. 320 ff.

2 T. W. Manson, MMW, p. 459; Lagrange, *op. cit.*, p. 321.

3 W. O. E. Oesterley, *The Jewish Background of the Christian
Liturgy* (1925).

4 Cf. I. Abrahams, *Pharisaism and the Gospels* (1924), Vol. II,
p. 98.

5 S-B, Vol. I, p. 407.

6 This bringing together of Deut. 6:4 and Lev. 19:18 is not new
with our Lord. The two commandments are brought together
in the Testaments of the Twelve Patriarchs at Issachar 5:2; 7:6;
Dan. 5:3. Lying behind this, however, are Micah 6:8 and Amos
5:15.

7 MJ, Vol. II, pp. 204 f.: " New in this period is the phrase ' Father
in heaven ' for God. It is to be observed that it is never ' *the* Father
in heaven ' . . . but always with the note of personal relation,
' *Our* Father in heaven.' The metonymy is very frequent, and
occurs in commonplace contexts as well as in connections where
it has an especial appropriateness."

8 Cf. Lagrange, *op. cit.*, p. 321, and MTS, pp. 95–100.

9 J. M. Creed, *The Gospel According to St. Luke* (1930), p. 156.

10 Ex. 20:24; 23:21; Deut. 12:5, 11; 14:23 f.; 16:2, 6, 11; 26:2;
I Kings 8:29; 9:3; 11:36; II Kings 21:4, 7.

11 John Bright, *The Kingdom of God* (1953), pp. 215 ff. and
245 ff.

12 In the Aramaic the idiom is *yoma den weyomahra*. Cf. MB, pp.
151 ff.

¹³ I am indebted to M. Black for the reference to Joüon, MB, p. 254.

¹⁴ H. H. Rowley, *The Relevance of Apocalyptic* (1952), pp. 156 f.

Chapter XII

¹ MB, pp. 135 f.
² S-B, Vol. I, pp. 429 f. and Tobit 4:8 ff.; Ps. Sal. 9:5; Apoc. Bar. 24:1; 4 Ezra 8:36.
³ Strack-Billerbeck have at this point perhaps the best comment which may be made, namely, that the Greek *haplous* ("single") is to be understood in the light of the contrasting adjective *poneros* ("sickly" or "poor"). They suggest that probably the Aramaic *sheˡlim* ("perfect") may stand behind the Greek *haplous*. Accepting this suggestion, we have translated the adjectives respectively "clear" and "clouded." S-B, Vol. I, p. 431.
⁴ MB, p. 102, and S-B, Vol. I, p. 434.
⁵ MB, p. 76.
⁶ Cf. my *Prophetic Realism and the Gospel* (1955), pp. 169–172.
⁷ M. Black has suggested that Luke's "ravens" at ch. 12:24 gives us a better word play than Matthew's "birds," *op. cit.*, p. 136. My translation of "wild country lilies" and "wild country reed" represents a suggestion of the same author in a note on MB, p. 96. For the translation "the rest of men" at v. 32, cf. my comment above on Matt. 6:5 and MB, pp. 133 f.
⁸ MMW, p. 465.

Chapter XIII

¹ John Knox, *The Man Christ Jesus* (1941), p. 42.
² Cf. my discussion of this matter in *The Religion of Maturity* (1948), p. 196.
³ MJ, Vol. I, pp. 494 ff.
⁴ S-B, Vol. I, p. 443.
⁵ *Ibid.*, p. 446.
⁶ MJ, Vol. II, p. 193.
⁷ MB, pp. 146 ff., 211. Black proceeds to give a further modification of the saying which I think is less acceptable, to the effect that it should read as follows: "Hang not (precious) rings on dogs, Adorn not the snout of swine with your pearls."

Chapter XIV

1 MB, pp. 44 ff.
2 *Ibid.*, pp. 34 ff.
3 *Ibid.*, pp. 235 f.
4 Irenaeus, *Against Heresies*, III, 25, 3.
5 See Claude G. Montefiore's vigorous — and, on the whole, convincing — defense of this thesis in *The Old Testament and After* (1923), pp. 11 ff.
6 Deut. 4:37; I Kings 10:9; Ps. 23:1; 48:9; 51:1; 89:1–4; 106:1; Isa. 43:4; Jer. 31:3; Hos. 11:1; Mal. 1:2.
7 S-B, Vol. I, p. 450.
8 MMW, p. 373.
9 *Ibid.*, p. 373
10 MTS, p. 307.

Chapter XV

1 CAP, Vol. II, p. 262.
2 For other references to the doctrine see Ecclus. 15:17; 17:6; Test. Asher 1:3, 5; II Peter 2:2; Didache 1:1; Sibyll. Oracles 8:399 f.
3 Theodor H. Gaster, *The Dead Sea Scriptures*, pp. 62, 76, 117, 141, 144.
4 For an excellent presentation of the whole problem of supra-normal experience and " false prophets," see H. H. Rowley, *The Old Testament and Modern Study* (1951), pp. 134 ff.; John Skinner, *Prophecy and Religion* (1951), pp. 185 ff. Incidentally, the phrase *nebhie d^{e}shuqre* gives us a nice rhyme with *bal^{e}bhusha d^{e}emre*, which is found in the next line in the Syr ^{cur} for " in the clothing of sheep."
5 At a later day in the history of the Christian church, the church had to battle with such political opportunists as Judas Magus (Acts 13:6).
6 S-B say that they find none anywhere. This is fair evidence that there is none such. S-B, Vol. I, p. 465.
7 In addition to the obvious parallel construction in these five lines, there are at least two clear Aramaisms: the " impersonal verb " in the expression " they do not gather " (MB, p. 91), and the Aramaic behind the several uses of the verb " yield " (*ibid.*, pp. 101, 148 f.).

8 See the phrase "day of the Lord" in Ps. 96:13; 98:9; Dan. 12:2; Amos 5:18, 20; Zeph. 1:14–16; Joel 2:31 f.; Zech. 14:6.

9 M. Black suggests that the reading of the Syr cur, which has "walked" instead of "taught" at this point, is perhaps original (MB, p. 187).

10 In the first line of this stanza we have followed Luke's rendering "is . . . addressing me" at 6:46. As M. Black suggests this represents a better Aramaic idiom than that in Matthew (MB, pp. 236 and 276). S-B give a number of quotations from the rabbinical literature to indicate that a doubling of a name as in "Lord, Lord" and "Jerusalem, Jerusalem" was a common practice of the day (MB, p. 943).

11 S-B, Vol. I, p. 469.

12 The stanza contains a number of Aramaisms. Thus, the two expressions "I should compare" and "should be compared" probably stand for a sort of modal use of the Aramaic future (MB, p. 254).

Epilogue

1 MTS, p. 107.
2 S-B, Vol. I, p. 470.
3 *The Intention of Jesus*, p. 98.
4 See my *Prophetic Realism and the Gospel*, pp. 61 ff.

Scripture References

Names and Subjects

Abraham, 154
Adultery, 75 f., 82
Almsgiving, 111–114
"Approval seekers," 114
Aramatic expressions, 50 f.
Arrogance, spiritual, 128
Augustine, 71, 128

Barrett, C. K., 53
Barth, K., 42, 66, 76, 121
Beatitudes, 27 f., 37 ff.
Begging, 97
Black, M., 13, 51, 67, 95, 116, 126, 150
Blessed (*makarios*), 28 f.
Borrowing, 97
Bread, use of word, 126
Burney, C. F., 13, 95

Church, as body of Christ, 125
Creed, J. M., 123

Dead Sea scrolls, 69, 70, 159
Deissmann, A., 117
Deutero-Isaiah, 47, 154
Didache, 117, 129
Divorce, 80 f.

Easton, B. S., 17
Emotions, and emotional life, 99 f.
Eschatology, 42, 160, 161
Ethic,
    "absolute," 143
    Christian, 93, 105
    crossless, 94 f., 105
Evangelism, 43

Evil One, 88, 128
Exhibitionism, religious, 110, 114, 115, 117, 149, 162
Ezra, 111

Fasting, Pharisaic practice of, 116
Forgiveness, 32 f.
Future life, 79

Gehenna, 79
God,
    activity of, 53, 55
    consecration to, 131 f.
    image of, 69
    name of, 85 f., 124, 167
    as Providential Governor, 140
    reconciliation with, 127
    sovereignty of, 124 f., 141
    and wealth, 137, 138
    will of, 55 f., 163
Golden Rule, 105, 156
Goodspeed, E., 29

Holy Spirit, 153, 167

Ignatius, 48

Jesus' teaching,
    themes of, 47, 65, 74
    effectiveness of, 165 ff.
Jülicher, A., 12

Kingdom of God, 31 f., 42, 124, 125, 163
Knox, John, 143

187